The Spokesı

Think Globally, Act

Edited by Tony Sim

Published by Spokesman ıor ıne
Bertrand Russell Peace Foundation
Ken Coates: Editor 1970 to 2010

Spokesman 128 2015

CONTENTS

Cartoon: with grateful thanks to Steve Bell

ISSN 1367 7748 Printed by the Russell Press Ltd., Nottingham, UK ISBN 978 0 85124 847 9

ıs
:38.00
:38.00 (Europe)
:33.00 (UK)
:20.00 (UK)
£25.00 (ex UK)

A CIP catalogue record for this book is available from the British Library

Published by the
Bertrand Russell Peace
Foundation Ltd.,
Russell House
Bulwell Lane
Nottingham NG6 0BT
England
Tel. 0115 9784504
email:
elfeuro@compuserve.com
www.spokesmanbooks.com
www.russfound.org

The Ken Coates Memorial Lecture

THE FUTURE OF THE LEFT - where next for Britain's labour movement?

with Frances O'Grady

Frances O'Grady, General Secretary of the Trades Union Congress, will give the inaugural Ken Coates Memorial Lecture at the **University of Nottingham**.

WEDNESDAY 3RD JUNE
6.30PM

The Law and Social Sciences building,
University Park Campus,
Nottingham NG7 2RD

FREE ENTRY

For booking and registration, please email **tonysimpson@russfound.org**

Editorial

Think Globally, Act Locally

In 1988, Ken Coates published a book under the same title as this editorial, in which he argued, with characteristic democratic emphasis, for a UN popular consultative assembly (see excerpt below). The timing was significant. The year before, the Intermediate-Range Nuclear Forces (INF) Treaty had been signed by General Secretary Gorbachev and President Reagan, outlawing a whole class of nuclear weapons. This landmark agreement represented the high water mark of European Nuclear Disarmament, to which Ken had dedicated much of his life and work during the preceding decade. The following year, 1989, he was elected to the European Parliament for the first time, and quickly became the President of its Human Rights Sub-committee.

We revisit END through Ken's audacious proposal for a 'joint session' of the European Parliament and the Supreme Soviet. This is a record of dead hopes but far-from-dead fears, as the bloody confrontation currently centred on Ukraine reminds us. Richard Sakwa provides much needed insight and objectivity in the otherwise slanted public commentary on Russia-Ukraine-NATO-European Union relations. His conclusions echo earlier concerns:

> 'If Europe is not once again to be divided, there need to be new ideas about what an inclusive and equitable political and security order encompassing the whole continent would look like. In other words, the idea of Greater Europe needs to be endowed with substance and institutional form.'

The collapse of the Soviet Union, in 1991, rendered futile any plans for joint sessions between the Supreme Soviet and the European Parliament. But, decades later, enduring peace on the Eurasian landmass requires a change of direction away from treating Russia as the 'enemy', towards building our 'common European home'.

We also reprint the transcript of Ken Coates' address to trade unionists, entitled 'From a mob to a movement'. Different from his written style, Ken's fluency in speaking to such audiences is evident from the text. The occasion was a study day at Nottingham University in June 1991, the year the first part of the official *History of the Transport and General Workers' Union* was published to critical acclaim. Co-authored with Tony Topham, Ken regarded the *History* as a high point in his long list of publications. Regrettably, the second part of the *History,* post 1922, was never completed, as work in the European Parliament made increasingly heavy demands. Nevertheless, the totality of Ken's work is considerable, and Tom Unterrainer is compiling a comprehensive bibliography to supplement the archive in Nottingham University's Special Collections.

So it is fitting that the inaugural Ken Coates Memorial Lecture should be given by Frances O'Grady, General Secretary of the Trade Union Congress, at Nottingham University on 3 June 2015, some five years after Ken died, and shortly after the UK's General Election. Her theme is 'The Future of the Left: Where Next for Britain's Labour Movement?' We print Frances's comments on the implications for Europe of Syriza's anti-austerity campaign and the need for European policies which promote growth and employment, which were made in anticipation of Syriza's election victory in January, together with the TUC's considered support for Greek workers.

Ken's consistently 'global' outlook he shared with Bertrand Russell, with whom he worked closely for the last years of Russell's long and eventful life. Russell had come to Ken's aid when he was being expelled from the Labour Party for the first time, in the mid-1960s, mainly because of his outspoken opposition to the Vietnam War. *The Week*, 'a news analysis for socialists', was edited by Ken from Greenfield Street, next to the Nottingham University campus, and duplicated on machines elsewhere in the City. Its global perspective is immediately apparent, but so is its local grounding. There was extensive coverage of a long strike at Raleigh Cycles, for example, as well as disputes at hosiery factories in Long Eaton. It is in that spirit that this issue of *The Spokesman*, dedicated to Ken Coates and his political legacy, includes some local news of current attacks on the National Health Service in Nottingham, and the campaigns against them.

Tony Simpson

* * *

Ken Coates wrote:

'… supposing in the modern age that every six million adults in the world were to be invited to choose a representative for such a world forum, this could imply a process of election in which all the key issues would be extensively discussed. Parties would gell to express the different options, and many concealed options would be opened up. The press and television services would shift their attention, for a vital if brief period, to a global agenda ... national democratic forces would quickly discover their most appropriate international partners in dialogue and joint action. Linkages would emerge quickly and by rational choice rather than haphazardly and in the light of restricted and sometimes false information ... '

Think Globally, Act Locally, Spokesman Books, 1988

Europe's civil war

Richard Sakwa

In 2014, history returned to Europe with a vengeance. The crisis over Ukraine brought back not only the spectre but the reality of war, on the 100th anniversary of a conflict that had been spoken of as the war to end all war. The great powers lined up, amid a barrage of propaganda and informational warfare, while many of the smaller powers made their contribution to the festival of irresponsibility. This was also the 75th anniversary of the beginning of the Second World War, which wreaked so much harm on central and eastern Europe. The fall of the Berlin Wall 25 years earlier and the subsequent end of the Cold War had been attended by expectations of a Europe 'whole and free'. These hopes were crushed in 2014, and Europe is now set for a new era of division and confrontation. The Ukrainian crisis was the immediate cause, but this only reflected deeper contradictions in the pattern of post-communist development since 1989. In other words, the European and Ukrainian crises came together to devastating effect.

The 'Ukrainian crisis' refers to profound tensions in the country's nation and state-building processes since it achieved independence in late 1991, which now threaten the unity of the state itself. These are no longer described in classical ideological terms, but, in the Roman manner, through the use of colours. The Orange tendency thinks in terms of a Ukraine that can finally fulfil its destiny as a nation state, officially monolingual, culturally autonomous from other Slavic nations and aligned with 'Europe' and the Atlantic security community. This is a type of 'monism', because of its emphasis on the

Richard Sakwa is Professor of Russian & European Politics at University of Kent. We are grateful for his permission to run this excerpt from his timely new book, Frontline Ukraine: Crisis in the Borderlands *(IB Tauris, £18.99). Jonathan Steele reviews* Frontline Ukraine *elsewhere in this issue.*

singularity of the Ukrainian experience. By contrast, Blue has come to symbolise a rather more plural understanding of the challenges facing Ukraine, recognising that the country's various regions have different historical and cultural experiences, and that the modern state needs to acknowledge this diversity in a more capacious constitutional settlement. For the Blues, Ukraine is more of a 'state nation', an assemblage of different traditions, but above all one where Russian is recognised as a second state language and economic, social and even security links with Russia are maintained. Of course, the Blue I am talking about is an abstraction, not the blue of former president Viktor Yanukovych's Party of Regions. The Blues, no less than the Orangists, have been committed to the idea of a free and united Ukraine, but favour a more comprehensive vision of what it means to be Ukrainian. We also have to include the Gold tendency, the powerful oligarchs who have dominated the country since the 1990s, accompanied by widespread corruption and the decay of public institutions. Since independence, there has been no visionary leader to meld these colours to forge a Ukrainian version of the rainbow nation.

The 'Ukraine crisis' also refers to the way that internal tensions have become internationalised to provoke the worst crisis in Europe since the end of the Cold War. Some have even compared its gravity with the Cuban missile crisis of October 1962. The world at various points stood close to a new conflagration, provoked by desperately overheated rhetoric on all sides. The asymmetrical end of the Cold War effectively shut Russia out from the European alliance system. The failure to establish a genuinely inclusive and equal security system on the continent imbued European international politics with powerful stress points, which in 2014 produced the international earthquake that we now call the Ukraine crisis. There had been plenty of warning signs, with Boris Yeltsin, the Russian Federation's first leader, in December 1994 already talking in terms of a 'Cold Peace'. When he came to power in 2000, the Russian President, Vladimir Putin, devoted himself to overcoming the asymmetries. The major non-state institution at the heart of the architecture of post-communist Europe, the European Union (EU), exacerbated the tensions rather than resolving them. The EU represents the core of what could be called 'Wider Europe' – a Brussels-centric vision that extends into the heartlands of what had once been an alternative great-power system centred on Moscow. The increasing merger of Wider Europe with the Atlantic security system only made things worse.

Russia and some European leaders proposed not so much an alternative but a complementary vision to the monism of Wider Europe, known as

'Greater Europe': a way of bringing together all corners of the continent to create what Mikhail Gorbachev in the final period of the Soviet Union had called the Common European Home. This is a multipolar and pluralistic concept of Europe, allied with but not the same as the Atlantic community. In Greater Europe there would be no need to choose between Brussels, Washington or Moscow. In the absence of the tensions generated by the post-Cold War 'unsettlement', the peace promised at the end of the Cold War would finally arrive. Instead, the double 'Ukrainian' and 'Ukraine' crises combined with catastrophic consequences.

For me, this is both personal and political. The Cold War division of Europe is the reason I was born and grew up in Britain and not in Poland, but, even before that, war and preparations for war had scarred my family. In the inter-war years my father, an agronomist by profession but like so many of his generation also a reservist in the Polish army, marched up and down between Grodno and Lwów (as it was then called). He told of the 25kg he had to carry in his backpack, with all sorts of equipment and survival tools. The area at the time was part of the Second Polish Republic, and for generations had been settled by Poles. These were the *kresy*, the borderlands of Europe grinding up against the ever-rising power of the Russian Empire. With the partition of Poland in the 18th century, Grodno and what is now the western part of Belarus was ceded to Russia, while Lemberg (the German name for Lwów) and the surrounding province of Galicia became part of the Austro-Hungarian Empire. On gaining independence in 1918, and with Russia and the nascent Ukrainian state in the throes of revolution and civil war, the various armies repeatedly marched back and forth across the region. In the end the Polish state occupied an enormous territory to the east of the Curzon Line.

These were the lands occupied by Joseph Stalin, following the division of the area according to the Molotov–Ribbentrop Pact of 23 August 1939. Poland was invaded on 1 September and against the overwhelming might of Adolf Hitler's armies the Polish forces fell back, only for the Soviet Union to invade on 17 September.

My father's unit soon came up against the Soviet forces, and when greeted initially by the Poles as coming to support them against the Germans, they were asked to disarm. My father escaped to Hungary, but many of his reservist comrades were captured, and eventually murdered in Katyn and other killing sites.

My father subsequently joined the Polish Second Corps under General Anders, and with the British Eighth Army fought at El Alamein, Benghazi, Tobruk and then all the way up Italy, spending six months at Monte

Cassino. At the end of the war Poland was liberated, but it was not free. Unable to return to their homeland, the family was granted refuge in Britain. In the meantime, the Soviet borders were extended to the west, and Lwów became Lvov. These were territories that had never been part of the Russian Empire, and when Ukraine gained independence in 1991 they became the source of the distinctive Orange vision of Ukrainian statehood. Today Lvov has become Lviv, while its representation of what it means to be Ukrainian is contested by other regions and communities, notably the Blues, each of which has endured an equally arduous path to become part of the modern Ukrainian state.

As for the political, being a product of an ideologically and geographically divided Europe, I shared the anticipation at the end of the Cold War in 1989-91 that a new and united Europe could finally be built. For a generation the EU helped transcend the logic of conflict in the western part of the continent by binding the traditional antagonists, France and Germany, into a new political community, one that expanded from the founding six that signed the Treaty of Rome in March 1957 to the 28 member states of today. The Council of Europe, established in 1949, broadened its activities into the post-communist region, and now encompasses 47 nations and 820 million citizens, as its website proudly proclaims. The European Convention of Human Rights and its additional protocols established a powerful normative framework for the continent, policed by the European Court of Human Rights, based in Strasbourg. Russia in the 1990s actively engaged with the EU, signing a Partnership and Cooperation agreement in 1994, although it only took effect on 30 October 1997 following the first Chechen war, and the next year Russia joined the Council of Europe.

However, another dynamic was at work, namely the enlargement of the North Atlantic Treaty Organisation (NATO). Also established in 1949 to bring together the victorious western allies, now ranged against the Soviet Union in what had become the Cold War, NATO was not disbanded when the Soviet Union disintegrated and the Cold War came to an end. This was the source of the unbalanced end to the Cold War, with the eastern part dissolving its alliance system while NATO in the 1990s began a march to the east. This raised increasing alarm in Russia, and, while notionally granting additional security to its new members, it meant that security in the continent had become divisible. Worse, there was an increasing perception that EU enlargement was almost the automatic precursor to NATO expansion. There was a compelling geopolitical logic embedded in EU enlargement. For example, although many member states had reservations about the readiness of Bulgaria and Romania to join, there was a fear that they could drift off and become western versions of Ukraine. The project of European economic integration, and its associated peace project, effectively merged with the Euro-Atlantic security partnership, a fateful elision that undermined the rationale of both and which in the end provoked the Ukraine crisis.

The failure to create a genuinely inclusive and symmetrical post-communist political and security order generated what some took to calling a 'new Cold War', or, more precisely, a 'cold peace', which stimulated new resentments and the potential for new conflicts. It became increasingly clear that the demons of war in Europe had not been slain. Instead, the Ukraine crisis demonstrates just how fragile international order has become, and how much Europe has to do to achieve the vision that was so loudly proclaimed, when the Berlin Wall came down in November 1989, of a continent united from Lisbon to Vladivostok. The Ukraine crisis forces us to rethink European international relations. If Europe is not once again to be divided, there need to be new ideas about what an inclusive and equitable political and security order encompassing the whole continent would look like. In other words, the idea of Greater Europe needs to be endowed with substance and institutional form. Unfortunately, it appears that the opposite will happen: old ideas will be revived, the practices of the Cold War will, zombie-like, come back to life, and once again there will be a fatal dividing line across Europe that will mar the lives of the generation to come. This is far from inevitable, but to avoid it will require a shift in the mode of political intercourse from exprobration to diplomacy, and from denunciation to dialogue.

Thus the personal and the political combine, and *Frontline Ukraine* is as much an exploration of failed opportunities as it is an account of how we created yet another crisis in European international politics on the anniversaries of the start of two world wars and a moment of hope in 1989. My father's generation suffered war, destruction and displacement, and yet the European civil war that dominated the 20th century still inflames the political imagination of the 21st.

Common home

Ken Coates

Ken Coates was first elected Member of the European Parliament for Nottingham in 1989 and he served two terms, finishing in 1999. Previously, he had been unsuccessful as the Labour Party candidate in 1984, and in 1983, when he stood for Westminster in the Nottingham South constituency. Throughout the 1980s, he argued for European Nuclear Disarmament, and the creation of nuclear-weapons-free zones. This campaign achieved some success, with the removal and banning of intermediate-range nuclear forces under the INF Treaty of 1987, signed by Presidents Gorbachev and Reagan. But the political developments to safeguard Europe from future conflicts remained unaccomplished. With this in mind, and in the context of President Gorbachev's call for a 'common European home', Ken Coates explained why the European Parliament should meet the Supreme Soviet. This audacious proposal to unite East and West, which resonates strongly during current bloody confrontations, was set out in the first issue European Labour Forum, *a journal which he founded and edited in 1990.*

* * *

Every new day creates unforeseen choices for Europe. In both its Eastern and Western halves, our continent is becoming familiar with a new dimension of crisis. We are informed that when the Chinese write this word, they combine two other ideographs. 'Crisis', thus, contains in itself the concept of 'danger', but also that of 'opportunity'.

Understanding the danger, this complex combination explains why I proposed, six months ago, to try to make an opportunity.

My suggestion was that the two largest emerging democracies of East and West should arrange a suitable meeting. Separately, they were doing similar things. The European Parliament was seeking to prepare a democratic foundation for political union, at the same time that the Supreme Soviet considered how to lay out the groundwork for political pluralism and the rule of law. Each of us, I thought, had something to say to the other. We could help one another. Together, we might build more surely than we could apart. Even if they rejected the notion of 'common home', surely, I thought, colleagues might see advantage in ensuring that the structure we were seeking to erect could be safer if it were at least semi-detached! And if we talked, might we not see how to improve the architecture? In My Father's House are many mansions …

A mark of the speed of change is that the frank expression of disbelief, which often came across the faces of those who heard this proposal when first I made it, is now seldom seen. In the beginning perhaps half of my Western interlocutors thought I was crazy. Now, that number is well down. Of course, in truth, the hope for genuine European unity may really be crazy, but if it is, then we must at least observe that the world is going with it. In short order, first Poland, then Hungary, then the German Democratic Republic and Bulgaria, then Czechoslovakia and, latest, Romania, all embarked on the search for new political frameworks. Are they to be forever separate?

Some of the people who sought to dissuade us from any joint Parliamentary exchange with the Soviets were arguing, only a month or two ago, that the European Parliament should only meet with fully pluralist legislatures, and that Article Six of the Soviet Constitution precludes the development of any such openness. But now Article Six is on its way out. No one can be certain of continuity in any political process, as present events certainly argue. But how much further evidence is required before we open our eyes to what is happening? We have one sign after another, following so fast that one has to run to see them all: what new doubts can be invented to justify repudiation of what all of us know to be true? The present Soviet administration is trying to introduce major democratic reforms. It may be frustrated in the effort, but that effort is real. If we could help it, would we not be insane to refrain?

Another argument in Strasbourg was, initially, that perhaps it might be inconvenient to our Soviet partners to join in such a collaboration as that proposed. Then Mr Schevardnadze visited us, and said he would be willing to be present at a joint meeting. I visited Mr Zagladin, shortly afterwards, and he offered a careful four-point programme of stages for its realisation.

On my return I briefed Mr Vinci, the European Parliament's Secretary-General, on this conversation. He received the information with great interest, and was obviously intrigued by it. How is it possible still to argue that the project is too difficult, too uncertain, too expensive?

The original proposal suggested that preparations be undertaken by joint Committee sessions, pairing off the appropriate bodies of both Parliaments. If the preparatory work took two years, perhaps each joint Committee would meet twice, once in Brussels and once in Moscow. If appropriate, smaller subgroups might deal with specific problems. Some agreements, for ratification in joint plenum, would be easy to reach: exchanges of documents, information, trainees, for instance. Others could be more difficult.

But inter-committee collaboration is a functional exercise, and the Committees of both Parliaments are well-used to methodical and efficient work. It would not be beyond their powers to determine what could appropriately be tabled on their joint agenda. Some Committees have more to learn from one another than others. Some are already involved in overtures, one to another. None of this framework of activity involves superhuman fears of organisations, funding, or control.

A joint plenary might be slightly more difficult. However, using our powers of improvisation, it could be arranged at Strasbourg, or in any one of a dozen European cities. Whilst the costs would not be negligible, they would certainly be rapidly outweighed by the benefits.

What, in fact, could be done by joint East-West action, to resolve present problems?

The first phase of crisis, in Eastern Europe and the USSR, involves the political collapse of authoritarian systems, and the difficult search for democratic renewal. It has provoked, and is partially reinforced by, national tensions and economic imbalances. At another level, indebtedness aggravates social distress to a point which drives national differences beyond democratic resolution, into xenophobia. Without economic co-operation on a large scale, we risk the disaggregation of societies whose economies are falling down.

A deeper crisis is all too likely to arrive. The global disproportions between rich and poor nations have developed an unbelievable pattern of debt. The United States, which, after the Second World War, was powerful enough to initiate the Marshall Plan for European Recovery, and to impose the dollar as an international currency, is, today, the world's largest debtor nation. The potent Japanese economy operates on a global scale, but has not generated political institutions which can think globally, or any other than the defensive plan. More precisely, Japanese investors can go anywhere to close a barrier or make a space: but overall economic policy is reactive, not initiative. In the European Community there could, perhaps, arise a group of statesman with the vision and the skill to convene a new Bretton Woods conference, to tackle the problems involved in creating a new international economic order, a new world currency, and effective measures to unravel the bonds of debt. Would this not be easier with the help of the Soviet Union?

Superimposed on any Western economic crisis will be the problems of disarmament and development. If economic activity is not reoriented, disarmament will contribute to the circle of decline and contraction. If world trade is about to enter a phase of stringent compression, we may well be standing on the brink of trade wars. Less propitious conditions for major democratic reforms could scarcely be envisaged. The common sense answer speaks of converting military investments to civilian purposes. But then, common sense finds the notion of economic crisis difficult to comprehend …

It may be that current falls in commodity prices are only a 'blip'. It may be that pessimism about the Western economies is unfounded. In such a case, the arguments for joint efforts towards democracy, East and West, would stand or fall solely on their political merit. Is it not sensible, when one is embarking on a road of reform, to go along together? In which ways, by what devices, might we help one another? Are there any reasons which would justify ignoring each other's efforts, or even, undermining them? Should we listen to such reasons for *raisons d'état*, or discount them as immoral?

Perhaps, though, the economic wolf is really at our doors. If he is, co-operation takes on a special urgency.

The new global framework is unlikely to function if it is directed against a particular interest, to benefit a section of mankind. If we found how to redistribute resources in order to expand circulation, encourage sustainable development, focus resources to undo environmental damage, and open a total war on poverty, would this not also benefit the richest nations?

This seems to me to be the agenda of the 'common home'. Others might have a broader vison. Not the least of the virtues of the proposal for a joint meeting between the European Parliament and the Supreme Soviet lies in the fact that it stimulates people to enquire, what might this agenda be?

These plans collapsed with the demise of the Soviet Union in 1991, although the need for co-operation in our common European home did not.

PENGUIN CLASSICS

The Penguin Book of Russian Poetry

Edited by ROBERT CHANDLER,
BORIS DRALYUK and IRINA MASHINSKI

Russia's Poetry

The Penguin Book of Russian Poetry *(2015, £12.99) seeks to open up 'the world of Russian poetry to English readers for the first time'. Yet, in his insightful introduction, editor Robert Chandler acknowledges important guides, including his two Russian-American co-editors, Boris Dralyuk and Irina Mashinski, as well as Dimitri Obolensky's bilingual* Penguin Book of Russian Verse, *to which Chandler has turned 'many times since I first started learning Russian forty-five years ago'. Perhaps Penguin should consider a new edition of Obolensky's pioneering work, first published in the 1960s?*

Meanwhile, The Penguin Book of Russian Poetry, *structured around Pushkin's towering achievement, stretches back to Derzhavin and Krylov in the Eighteenth Century, features a dozen poets of the Nineteenth Century, including Tyutchev and Fet, and fifty or so from the Twentieth Century, including Tsvetaeva and Tarkovsky. Andy Croft contributes a Byronic salute to the Moscow Metro, by way of extra-Russian perspective.*

Good translations grow all the more precious in the age of Google Translate. 'Translation is an art,' says Chandler, 'and there is more than one way to go about it'. His inclination is to favour translations that use metre and rhyme – or at least hint at them – when the original uses metre and rhyme. 'Form,' he believes, 'matters.'

This is a lively collection complete with informative pen portraits such as that for Maximilian Voloshin, from which we reprint excerpts. It embraces the sweep of modern Russian history, including the now somewhat neglected Soviet period, imparting something of the profundity, humanity and suffering of that experience, whilst remaining upbeat and amusing, in the best traditions of Russian art.

Tony Simpson

* * *

Agitating in the Library

Maximilian Voloshin (1877-1932)

Born in Kiev, Maximilian Alexandrovich Voloshin spent much of his childhood in the Crimea. He studied at Moscow University but was expelled for subversive political activities – or as he put it, 'agitating in the library'. In the early 1900s, already known as a Symbolist poet and art critic, he moved between Paris, Moscow and St Petersburg. From 1907 he spent much of his time in the Crimea, settling there in 1916. For over a decade his large house in Koktebel, where he both wrote and painted, was a refuge for writers and artists of all political and artistic persuasions. Among his hundreds of guests were Gorky, Gumilyov, Osip and Nadezhda Mandelstam and Marina Tsvetaeva. In 1924 the house became a 'House of Creativity' for Soviet writers, the first of the many such closed-access hotels that became a central part of the Soviet cultural world …

… After an account of Voloshin saving a woman poet from execution, Teffi ends: 'In Novorossiisk, in Yekaterinodar, in Rostov-on-Don I would again encounter the light cloak, the gaiters and the round beret crowning the tight curls. On each occasion I heard sonorous verse being declaimed to the accompaniment of little squeals from women with flushed, excited faces. Wherever he went, Voloshin was using the hum – or boom – of his verse to rescue someone whose life was endangered.'

During the Red Terror following the evacuation of the White Army from the Crimea, Voloshin showed still greater courage. His belief in the power of his words – what Marianna Landa refers to as 'his Dostoevskian faith in the divine spark in the soul of the abominable criminal, and his Symbolist belief in the magic of the poetic word' – seems to have been unshakeable; his personal appeals to Red and White officials and commanders, on behalf of individuals, and his verse-prayers addressed to God, on behalf of his country, have much in common. Voloshin believed he could affect the course of events – and sometimes he did. That he escaped arrest and execution is astonishing.

From Civil War

And from the ranks of both armies –
the same voice, the same refrain:
'He who is not with us is against us.
You must take sides. Justice is ours.'

And I stand alone in the midst of them,
amidst the roar of fire and smoke,
and pray with all my strength for those
who fight on this side, and on that side.

(1919)

Translated by Robert Chandler

Terror

The working day started at night.
Denunciations, papers, certificates.
Death sentences signed in a hurry.
Yawning, drinking of wine

Vodka, all day, for the soldiers.
Come evening, by candlelight,
time to read out lists, herd
men and women into a dark yard,

remove shoes, clothes, underwear,
tie the stuff in bundles, pile
it up in carts, take the carts away,
share out rings and watches.

Nightfall, men and women forced
barefoot, naked, over ice-covered stones,
into waste ground outside town,
in wind from the north east.

Rifle-butted to the edge of a gully.
The lantern light wavering.
Machine-gunned for half a minute;
finished off with bayonets.

Into a pit, some not quite dead.
A covering of soil, in a hurry.
And, with a broad-flowing Russian song –
back into town, back home.

At dawn wives; mothers; dogs
made their way to the same gullies;
dug the ground; fought over bones;
kissed the flesh they held dear.

(26 April 1921, Simferopol)
Translated by Robert Chandler

From a mob to a movement

Ken Coates

In June 1991, the TGWU Midlands Region and Nottingham University's Department of Adult Education convened a day school to mark the publication of The History of the Transport and General Workers' Union. *It was addressed by Ken Coates and Tony Topham, authors of what became, in its paperback edition,* The Making of the Labour Movement: The Foundation of the Transport and General Workers' Union 1870-1922 *(Spokesman £11.99). We reprint Ken's remarks that day, which read as though they have been transcribed from a recording. Tony Topham's address, 'Unity in Diversity', can be found in* One Big Union *(Spokesman, £6).*

Why bother with history? Why, above all, bother with one thousand pages of history, which stops seventy years ago? Perhaps the best way to approach that is to try to draw for you a picture of what the allegedly unskilled workers, who gave us our subject matter, were like. How did they live, in the forgotten corners of Victorian Britain?

The fact of the matter is that in all British industrial towns, and above all, in the port cities, life was hell for the poorest people. It was calculated by sociologists, at the end of the century, that approximately one-third of the population of London was living in poverty, and by poverty they did not mean what modern sociologists mean. They mean dire and suffocating squalor. Poverty meant tenements in which sometimes five or ten people lived in one room. It meant courtyards where the water supply, such as it was, was shared between many such households. It meant privies that had to be emptied by the night soil man. London, for instance, in the last days at the end of nineteenth century Britain, had a whole tract of housing in the East End which was, as William Blake and Cobbett used to say in earlier days, 'a wen'. I am reminded of modern China when I look at those discrepancies between wealth and poverty. The West End, home of the lords of the earth, the owners of empire, people of unparalleled riches and ostentation, lay on one side. On the other was the East End crawling with vice, terrified by Jack the Ripper, an horrendous stew.

And what happened in those straitened circumstances? People normally have a certain capacity for supporting one another. People can normally be kindly, friendly and helpful, and there was, among these particular people, every need for all those resources of solidarity and decency, which the poorest of them could muster. But also, when one is competing for life, there are many instincts which pit people against each other. It can be a brutal struggle, each against all, for survival of those who are miscalled the fittest, which often means survival of the less conscientious and the least moral in the deprived population. All these things were mixed together; base and pure, mean and generous to a fault.

We do not try in *The History* to give you an idealised picture. Instead we try to recover the feel of those communities. The docks grew up in cities which had exploded in size, because the rail networks were decanting people in these vital areas at a rate far faster than the cities themselves could grow to assimilate them. Many or most of the people who were sucked into these growing urban areas were agricultural people. I have always thought it is a libel to say that such people were unskilled, but they had skills from a previous age. That is why so many of them became carters, because they knew about horses. Many others became dockers: many swapped roles, and many of the country people who did not actually migrate would find themselves drawn into the town after the harvest was in, which was when unemployment hit the agricultural labourers. Nearly always the docks had far more people wanting to work than could normally be given work. There were just rare moments when the weather was right, when the winds were right, when the demand was right, when the ships lined up to unload, that you could have something which fleetingly resembled full employment. Normally this was not so.

Work was organised quite differently in such places from the orderly rhythms we came to expect later in the car factories, which are so well understood and well remembered in the Midlands. The industrial discipline of this population that we are talking about hardly existed. People had come from the land, they had not become inured to the routine of the hooter and the clock, still less the drill of time study and careful managerial control. They queued up outside the dock gates and fought to get in. The foreman picked the fittest and set them on. The rest were sent away. They would go hungry.

So what are we talking about? Why have I gone into all this? I have gone into it because I want you to understand that everything that we take for granted today about trade unions was still unformed, unfixed: everything. We take for granted that there are and have always been working class people. Then, in the docks, there was a mob, when it all got together: and when it was not together there were tens of thousands of miserable individuals normally ground down into isolation, loneliness and poverty. Yet somehow or other those same people became a collective which was not a mob, no longer a bunch of social atoms either. They became something which today everybody assumes has always been with us, an independent-minded working class, with a self-confident working class movement. Banding those previously forlorn people together was actually the major breakthrough which created modern British democracy.

I know in school we were told it all started with the Magna Carta, 1215 and I don't know what. But actually at the time we are speaking about, the very large majority of British people had no say whatever about who were to become the politicians who might lead them. All women lacked the vote, but very large numbers of men also lacked the vote. There had been a big electoral reform in 1884, and the working class electorate had been increased. But it depended on various complex qualifications, according to household tenure, and there was the additional problem that middle class people commonly had two votes, because they could vote where they lived, and they could also vote where they held business property. That meant that you could not just take the electorate and do the sums and work out what the entitlement to political involvement was. And that is why, in the words of the old song,

'Every little Briton who's ever born alive,
is either a little Liberal or a little Conservative.'

The prosperous classes monopolised the vote. When you shared a tenement room in East London with all those other families, you lived in a world where things like voting could hardly be imagined.

And then suddenly, something happens. We see the outcast people associating themselves. Ben Tillett is one of the great heroes in this story, and what Ben Tillett says he did is very revealing. When he started work on the docks, having been a seaman, he took upon himself a stigma which made it impossible to confess where he was actually employed. Outside his work, when he was mixing in 'society', he would try to conceal what his job was. People who were doing his job were universally described as 'dock rats'. Ben Tillett claimed that he himself was the man who invented the word 'docker', which description marked a new beginning. It gave both self-respect and, yes, status to the job. But why were they seen, and why did they see themselves, as 'dock rats'? Because in order to get work, in attending the call-on, which was the selection of the fittest men to work those ships that were available for working, the men had, quite normally, to fight each other to be chosen. It was a raw, physical battle. There were innumerable descriptions of it, including lots by sociologists who began to visit and report at the time. It was a war. People's coats (and, said Tillett, sometimes even their ears) were torn off in the struggle to get to the gate and earn the pittance which was the difference between starvation – there was no welfare state – and a meagre livelihood. Sometimes men would be injured and maimed in the battle. All sorts of attempts were made to organise these people, and we have gone through those events in the book.

At the end of the 1880s, however, this whole submerged population exploded in a great rage of rebellion. It was started by the matchgirls who worked in Bryant and May's factory in Bow. They rebelled because they were levied a penny a week contribution, a compulsory tax put on them by the employer, an important Liberal, who demonstrated his party loyalty by building a statue of Gladstone, at the girls' expense, outside the factory. The girls were enraged by this, and in fact they mutinied when the statue was unveiled. There was a mob scene, when the girls threw themselves on the statue, and actually it got covered in blood where they had been beating it with their bare hands. So enraged were they all about the forced deduction of money to sustain a political cause which, they felt, had nothing to do with them. And yet it surely did have something to do with them, because they were the most exploited and suffocated group of people that you could ever meet. We have a picture of them in our book. Little waifs, they were, and they got all kinds of industrial diseases including the dreadful malady, 'phossy jaw', from the phosphorous used in the matches they made. This melts the bones. One of these children appeared in the House of Commons when the final strike broke out, and took her headscarf off, to the astonishment of the MPs, because all her hair had fallen out. Actually, that was the least of the problems, and many worse things than that happened. But that glimpse of Hell so shattered the MPs that they all declared themselves in support of the matchgirls. And when the East End of London was hit by this unlikely strike, it caused a tremendous amount of public concern. The truth about poverty and exploitation became momentarily visible to a more comfortable people. That lit a fire which spread out, so that there was a huge conflagration among first, the gasworkers, and then, the dockers. This was the movement which generated the great dock strike of 1889.

That dock strike was a fantastic event. It mobilised a hundred thousand people of East London, the poorest people not only on the docks, but all around them. They paraded through London day after day after day, and as they made their processions their grievances were paraded in the press. We had, in 1889, just entered the beginning of the age of the modern popular press, so those grievances presented themselves all over the country. So, indeed, did their rebellion. Suddenly you could see the poorest of the nation marching together and insisting that their complaints should be heard. In his way, all over the country, the dock strike was seen as a flame of rage and indignation, and of protest and hope. And now what did that do?

In history there are many examples of similar outbreaks, in which oppressed people have risen up and asserted themselves: and there are many of these examples – I could cite the history of some of the great strikes of the American labour movement, when after a year had gone by you could go back to see where that rebellion had been and find not a trace left of it. Nothing. People had vented their anger and then sunk back into quiescence.

But what the London dockers did was more than to rebel. They set out to create a union and to demand negotiations between the dockers and the port employers. A variety of other material demands were concerned: they are all recorded in *The History*. But all of them involved a new and central demand for recognition.

Recognition is the magic word. Its achievement, over time, did not just bring about collective bargaining: it also brought with it modern democracy. And that is why we must ask, what does recognition mean? There you had among the dock employers the most disreputable bunch of old feudal magnates that ever there was. They really were money-grubbing, grasping, backward-looking monsters. Against this grouping, the dockers' union, with the help of the Catholic Church in the person of Cardinal Manning, with the help of parts of the Liberal establishment, and with the help of the liberal press, notably the evening paper in London, *The Star*, managed to create such a pressure that even these, the most backward employers in the land, were compelled to negotiate. They were compelled to recognise that these workmen were no longer individual 'dock rats'. Now they were the Dockers' Union. You see what that means: first of all, it means the dockers had won their claims; secondly, it means the dockers could build their organisation; thirdly, and this is the key question, it means that the dockers could recognise their own unity, their community of interest, through its reflection in the eyes of their enemy. He *recognised* them. Their basic wage and conditions, then, came to depend upon their adversary's recognition that they had been agreed with the union.

So the men were a unity. I think that is a core element in the creation of modern democracy, because it meant that the poor, once they got the idea of union into their heads, even if the recognition was later taken away, had already experienced what was to become crucial to them: the knowledge that their individual strength would inevitably be the greater when they belonged to a collective in which they had confidence and trust. That is the basis upon which they began to organise, not only collective bargaining in industry, but also the long and difficult process which led to political representation.

Of course, political action became necessary because the people who were 'recognised' were a minority of the great population outside, clamouring for work. Although you could try to organise similar recognition for that wider population, and perhaps win many successes, it was a bit like baling out the ocean with a spoon. To make a substantial change, extending recognition to all who needed it, you had to get political representation and you had to get the vote. But to use that vote you also had to win a second recognition, expressing your own special political interests in distinction to those of the existing parties, representing the comfortable classes.

It wasn't an accident that the girls in Bryant and Mays rebelled about the statue of Gladstone. The Liberal employers were among the most persistent of all in exploiting the un-unionised labour forces and in driving down conditions. The same thing was the case in Brunner Mond, the forerunners of ICI; in one of our chapters we describe how Tom Mann became involved in a big effort to impose shorter hours and safe conditions in that enterprise. He had to adopt an alias, and smuggle himself into employment, so keen were these employers to keep out unions and all who might advance them.

Voting liberal, then, which was what such working class voters as there were were most commonly wont to do, was not going to advance their interests at work, because the same Liberals who stood on the hustings promising all kinds of benevolence were also the big employers who resisted unions. So there grew up a campaign for separate labour representation. Recognition, representation, these are all parts of the creation of an identity. It wasn't already there: it had to be made, it had to be built.

Of course, what happened was that the dock strike led directly to the election of the first really independent Labour MP, Keir Hardie, Member for West Ham, and also to the election of John Burns, who had played a key role in 1889, and of Havelock Wilson, the Seamen's leader. These political events arose directly from the organisation of the dockers and the surrounding transport and general workers, the gas workers, the people involved as carters and all the rest of them.

In turn, organisation led directly into local government representation, with the winning of Labour voices on the new local councils, first of all in the London area and then further afield. When Keir Hardie was elected, although he was not a docker, he became the political representative of the dockers' new unionism, and he was directly supported by the leaders of that process. Keir Hardie was elected three years after the great dock strike.

The year after that, in 1893, there met the first conference of the Independent Labour Party. It was called in Bradford. Who was the Parliamentary candidate of the ILP in Bradford? Who but our old friend Ben Tillett! Very soon afterwards, Tom Mann was selected as the Independent Labour candidate in Halifax.

When you ask why, what you find is that in Bradford, too, they had an immense strike, the Manningham Mills dispute. It had been caused by contraction in the textile industry resulting from trade protection in the United States. That strike itself created an enormous popular unity and rebellion in Bradford, but the Bradford people, including their leaders, looked towards the dockers' leaders, because those dockers' leaders had been advertised all over the country as near miracle-workers. These, after all, were the people who had turned the people of the East End from a lethargic and dispersed mass of individuals into a united fighting force. So, send for Ben Tillett, send for Tom Mann! And up they came to Yorkshire. Who better to choose as parliamentary candidates? But we should notice that they, too, were the people who sharpened the argument so that the ILP was actually begun, and within one year, Tom Mann, who was the dockers' President, had also become the General Secretary of the ILP.

I want to make it very plain that it was the struggle of these same leaders of the transport workers, which persuaded the TUC itself to go for shorter working hours by law, in the campaign for the legal eight hour day. This we still have not won. But it was these leaders who prepared the ground for the formation of the political Labour Party, the party we know today, and a key issue in that argument was that of working time. Shorter hours by law were not what Liberal employers wanted. So, in Parliament, they voted against. Everyone could then see what limits there were to liberal philanthropy.

At the turn of the century, it was the Liverpool dockers' leader, James Sexton, and the London dockers' leader, Ben Tillett, who joined forces with the railwaymen's union, to put down proposals at the TUC in 1899, ten years after the story began, to convene the conference which founded the Labour Party. Those three organisations met to composite their separate resolutions into a joint motion, under the chairmanship of Keir Hardie. This was then carried through the TUC, so that the conference that called the Labour Party into being was two-thirds the responsibility of the Transport and General Workers' forerunners, and one-third the responsibility of their allies in what later became the NUR.

Now why? The answer is that this political struggle was absolutely essential for the poorest people, because they lacked the monopoly position of skilled workers. They could not trade on their scarcity. Instead they had to secure some political intervention to make space for recognition.

Recognition was reinforced by government intervention, by the government holding the ring in industrial relations between the two sides. The government indeed made very tentative interventions in this process throughout the first part of this century. As time wore on, it made more and more strong appearances, culminating in a rush of government actions establishing a powerful presence during the First World War. But each intervention reinforced recognition, and therefore reinforced the sense of identity that workers got from seeing their unity reflected in the adversary's eyes. That is what made possible what happened after the First World War, the displacement of the Liberal Party by a Labour opposition led by Ramsay MacDonald.

None of that would have happened if there had been no successful move to organise the so-called unskilled workers. And all of it was a direct result of what? Of the inventive skills of these same dispossessed people.

The transport workers did not follow lamely behind the skilled workers, the aristocrats of labour. At the beginning of the trade union story, if you remember, there were some skilled workers' unions in which you would be fined for not going to the meeting. There were others in which you were not allowed into the meeting if you did not wear a tall silk hat, and a frock coat, and a bow tie. I am not exaggerating. The rules used to state you had to be 'properly dressed'. To be properly dressed, of course, cost an arm and a leg. When the first dockers' union delegates went to the TUC, there was a famous row because John Burns, that great spokesman of the dock strike who was elected as an MP in 1892, wrote an article in which he pointed out that the skilled workers were not only better turned out, but also all taller, stouter, better built, and smoother than these ragged individuals who now came in representing the dockers. Burns was accused of something close to racialism for saying this, but it was the sober truth.

As these people organised themselves, all their skills and all their inventiveness found an outlet. They were making and shaping a political process. That process led to the formation of the Labour Party, and it also led to the extension of the franchise. This became unavoidable during the First World War, because millions of voteless men were mown down to save 'their country'.

After conscription came in, it could not even be said they were volunteers. Clearly it was indefensible to be herded into war and slaughter without the right to vote on whether to support the hostilities or not. The call for male suffrage led to the universal franchise in which women were able to vote, and in which general elections could begin to register the actual opinions of the British population. And the first time that that happened was in the period immediately after the First World War. That is the date of British modern democracy, and you can say really that the whole of that process is covered in *The History*, and that there was, in fact, at the beginning of the story, no political democracy in this country, there was a club of the oligarchs, and at the end of the story rudimentary popular democracy was beginning to assert itself, and the people were beginning to find a way to express themselves.

At the forefront of that popular movement were the so-called unskilled workers, the lesser breeds, the ones with dirty hands, the ones who could not dress in the proper attire, the ones who were outside the pale. That's an extraordinary story!

People should be very proud of the traditions of the Transport and General Workers' Union. It is really the uncelebrated story of everything that is good in Britain. The last thing I should say is that in the processes which led to all these developments, there was a very important juncture.

You see, when you began to organise against the indifference and hostility of an enfranchised minority, you had to look which way you could go in order to express the democratic will, and among the people who joined the dockers' union the day after the great dock strike were two branches in Sweden, another branch in Holland. What were they doing? Port workers everywhere had the same interests. Seamen everywhere had the same interests. From the beginning, they saw their interests as involving a linkage, like with like. The workers had no country. They really did not have a country, they could not vote where they lived, they had no power there: but they had a common interest with other workers doing the same jobs that they were doing in another country, in which they, too, could not vote. Furthermore, if they all stood together, they could prevail, because they could impose recognition on all the employers in all the ports around the globe. The dockers during the dock strike would have been starved back to work if it had not been for the raising of tens of thousands of pounds by Australian trade unionists. This gave the impulse to an enormous movement of international support and solidarity.

What we tend not to see is that it also was a choice: were you going to organise nationally? In that case you had to organise a political party, and you had to win the vote. To cap that, you then had to win the electorate and you then had to go through all the political processes you understand. Or were you going to organise internationally? In that case you could create brand new institutions because there wasn't any international parliament. So you could 'do it yourself' by assembling an overwhelming force, which would mean that people would have to listen to the voices that you represented.

There was a long struggle between these two roads to democracy. It was finally resolved when the governments of Western Europe gave in to popular pressure and conceded the popular vote. To make this happen it took a world war in which millions of people were killed.

Our story has been completely different since then, because in every country, and above all in Britain, once we got the vote it meant that our main way forward was national, because we could organise, we could win elections, we could put people in the government, we could change the policy. Obviously common sense said that you combine collective bargaining and political mobilisation, and on the national plane that was your way forward. Of course, now we are coming round in a circle, because at the national plane we find we do all these things, and we win an election, and yet still we can't change anything, because all the industrial forces have now become international themselves, and they confront us with the kind of power that our unions never had, but that they were seeking to get, back at the end of the nineteenth century. They confront us with immense power, and we shan't win it back until we unite our forces at least as closely in order to be able to bargain for the people we represent, whether they live in Sicily or in Denmark or in Birmingham. That's a new agenda, a really powerful agenda, but it's an agenda which I think you get enormous help in meeting if you work through the experiences of our grandfathers and great-grandfathers in the story that we've been trying to tell. There is nothing new under the sun. Actually, this history is as much about tomorrow as it is about yesterday.

Red Cross Alert!

Peter Maurer

This year is the 70th anniversary of the atomic bombings of Hiroshima and Nagasaki – events that have left an indelible mark on humanity's conscience and consciousness.

I was in Hiroshima last week. I visited the Peace Memorial Museums and spoke to *hibakusha* – survivors. 70 years after the nuclear bombs were dropped on these cities, the lives of the survivors, the lives of countless people in Japan, are still overshadowed by these two watershed events in the history of modern warfare.

This year's 70th anniversary is a forceful reminder of the catastrophic and lasting human cost of nuclear weapons. It is a stark reminder of the incineration of two cities and their inhabitants. For the survivors, it is a reminder of the burns, blindness and blast injuries that went untreated because the medical infrastructure had been destroyed; of the slow and painful deaths; of the suffering endured by those who were exposed to radiation and, 70 years later, are still being treated for cancers and other diseases.

Seventy years ago, ICRC and Japanese Red Cross staff worked in unimaginable conditions to aid the victims and relieve the suffering caused by the atomic blasts. But how could we treat victims when hospitals had been reduced to rubble and ash and their medical supplies contaminated? The Japanese Red Cross Hospital, 1.5 kilometres from the hypocentre of the Hiroshima bomb, was somehow still standing after the explosion. There, doctors and nurses from the Japanese Red Cross did what they could. But it was clearly not enough to alleviate the suffering of those affected by the blast.

Peter Maurer is president of the International Committee of the Red Cross (ICRC). This is what he told the diplomatic community in Geneva in February 2015, following his visit to Hiroshima and Nagasaki.

Based on these experiences, the ICRC concluded as early as September 1945 that the humanitarian consequences of nuclear weapons were simply unacceptable. From a humanitarian perspective, nuclear weapons should be abolished. Later, the ICRC, along with the broader Red Cross and Red Crescent Movement, called on States to reach an agreement to prohibit nuclear weapons.

Throughout history, humanitarian disasters have often been the catalyst for the adoption of new laws to prevent further suffering, deaths and atrocities in war. One such example was the use of poison gas in the First World War, which led to the adoption of the 1925 Geneva Protocol and the subsequent banning of chemical and biological weapons.

Yet today, 70 years after Hiroshima and Nagasaki – names that recall humanitarian disasters like no other – clear progress towards the prohibition and elimination of nuclear weapons is lacking. Nuclear weapons are the one weapon of mass destruction on which we are still confronted with a legal gap.

We recognize the efforts that have been made and the fundamental importance of the Treaty on the Non-Proliferation of Nuclear Weapons (NPT) and all the commitments it contains, as well as other efforts to advance nuclear disarmament. But in light of the potential humanitarian consequences, progress in the field of disarmament is, as of now, insufficient.

Five years ago, my predecessor forcefully reiterated the ICRC's call for the non-use and elimination of nuclear weapons. The UN Security Council Summit and the US and Russian presidents had the previous year committed to 'create the conditions for a world without nuclear weapons'. We were heartened that, in May 2010, all NPT States Parties recognized, for the first time, the 'catastrophic humanitarian consequences of any use of nuclear weapons', and that nuclear-weapon States Parties committed to accelerating progress on the steps leading to nuclear disarmament and to undertaking further efforts to reduce and ultimately eliminate all types of nuclear weapons.

I have invited the diplomatic community back here today because the ICRC is gravely concerned that these undertakings are at risk.

In April 2015, the commitment to move towards a world without nuclear weapons is again to be addressed in the framework of the NPT Review Conference. This is a pivotal moment for the Treaty and for efforts to ensure that nuclear weapons are never again used. Much has happened since the last Review Conference. There are new developments and perspectives that the ICRC believes States must take into account as they prepare for the Conference and for any future work to address the dangers of nuclear weapons.

The Review Conference will have before it extensive and, in some areas, new information on the humanitarian consequences of nuclear weapons. Thanks to the conferences held in Oslo, Nayarit and Vienna, the international community now has a much clearer grasp of the risk that nuclear weapons might be used or accidentally detonated and the effects that such an event would have on people and societies around the globe, as well as on the environment. These conferences have confirmed and expanded what the ICRC learned from its experience in Hiroshima. Here are some of the key points that we take away from these meetings:

- Nuclear weapons are unique in their destructive power and in the scale of human suffering they cause. Their use, even on a limited scale, would have catastrophic and long-lasting consequences for human health, the environment, the climate, food production and socio-economic development.
- The health impacts of these weapons can last for decades and impact the children of survivors through genetic damage to their parents. This has been evident where nuclear weapons have been both used and tested. We could not have imagined that Japanese Red Cross hospitals would still be treating victims of cancer and leukaemia attributable to radiation from the atomic blasts – today, 70 years on.
- Seventy years after the dawn of the 'nuclear age,' there is no effective or feasible means of assisting a substantial portion of survivors in the immediate aftermath of a nuclear detonation, while adequately protecting those delivering assistance, in most countries or at the international level.
- The humanitarian consequences of a nuclear-weapon detonation would not be limited to the country where it occurs but would impact other countries and their populations. Thus, the continued existence of nuclear weapons and the risk of their intentional or accidental use is and must be a global concern.

Testimonies by nuclear experts and former nuclear force officers have shown that accidental nuclear-weapon detonations remain a very real danger. Malfunctions, mishaps, false alarms and misinterpreted information have nearly led to the intentional or accidental detonation of nuclear weapons on numerous occasions since 1945. The non-use of nuclear weapons over the past 70 years provides no assurance that such weapons will not be used in the future. Only the prohibition and elimination of nuclear weapons can prevent the severe humanitarian consequences that would entail.

In reality, the growing number of States that possess nuclear weapons and the potential for non-State actors to acquire them or related materials increases the risk of both deliberate and accidental detonations. The fact that an estimated 1,800 nuclear warheads remain on 'high alert' status, ready to be launched within minutes, further amplifies those risks. Calls since the end of the Cold War to reverse such policies have, unfortunately, gone unheeded.

The information acquired since the last NPT Review Conference has increased the ICRC's concerns about nuclear weapons. In our view, these findings have significant implications for the assessment of nuclear weapons under the fundamental rules of international humanitarian law. The new information about the health and environmental effects and the absence of an adequate assistance capacity in most countries should trigger a reassessment of nuclear weapons by all States in both legal and policy terms.

Already in 1996, in response to the Advisory Opinion of the International Court of Justice (see *Spokesman 63*), the ICRC concluded that 'it is difficult to envisage how any use of nuclear weapons could be compatible with the requirements of international humanitarian law'. The evidence that has emerged since only strengthens these doubts. With every new piece of information, we move further away from any hypothetical scenario where the humanitarian consequences of the use of nuclear weapons could be compatible with international humanitarian law. This leads us, time and again, to the conclusion that the use of nuclear weapons must be prohibited and the weapons eliminated altogether.

The ICRC believes that reducing the risk of nuclear-weapon use and ensuring their elimination through a legally binding international agreement is a humanitarian imperative. Significant steps have already been taken. States with the largest stockpiles of nuclear weapons have, since the end of the Cold War, significantly reduced the number of warheads that they possess. The 2010 New START treaty will further reduce the number of deployed nuclear weapons. Important steps have also been taken to increase security for nuclear materials. 115 States have signed treaties establishing nuclear-weapon-free zones and nearly all countries have committed to refrain from testing nuclear weapons by joining the Comprehensive Nuclear-Test-Ban Treaty or by establishing moratoria on nuclear testing.

However, other trends since 2010 give reason for grave concern. There is no evidence of negotiations for 'rapid reductions' of nuclear weapons and even fewer signs of momentum towards their 'total elimination'. Reports that the pace of reduction of nuclear arsenals has slowed and of the modernization of nuclear weapons by some States raise concerns that their role in security policies is not actually being reduced and may provide incentives for proliferation.

The 70th anniversary of the first use of nuclear weapons is the moment to signal that the era of nuclear weapons is coming to an end and that the threat of these weapons will be forever banished. It is the time to draw legal, political and operational conclusions from what has been learned about those 'catastrophic humanitarian consequences' that States party to the Non-Proliferation Treaty recognised five years ago.

In 2011, the Council of Delegates of the International Red Cross and Red Crescent Movement appealed to all States 'to ensure that nuclear weapons are never again used' and 'to prohibit the use of and completely eliminate nuclear weapons through a legally binding international agreement, based on existing commitments and international obligations'. I echo that call here today. The ICRC also appeals to States to fulfil the commitments contained in Article 6 of the NPT by establishing a time-bound framework to negotiate a legally binding agreement – and to consider the form that such an agreement could take. The catastrophic humanitarian consequences of nuclear weapons and current trends are too serious to ignore. The prohibition and elimination of these weapons through a legally binding agreement is the only guarantee that they will never be used again.

States Parties should make the NPT Review Conference in May 2015 a turning point for decision-making and progress in this area.

Until the very last nuclear weapon is eliminated, more also needs to be done to diminish the immediate risks of intentional or accidental nuclear detonations. We call on States that possess nuclear weapons and their allies to take further concrete steps to reduce the role and significance of nuclear weapons in their military plans, doctrines and policies. We urge nuclear-armed States to reduce the number of warheads on high alert and to be more transparent about action taken to prevent accidental detonations. Many of these steps derive from long-standing political commitments and multilateral action plans and should be followed through as a matter of urgency.

Protecting humanity from the catastrophic humanitarian consequences of nuclear weapons requires courage, sustained commitment and concerted action. Today's complex security environment highlights both the challenges and necessity of such action. Nuclear weapons are often presented as promoting security, particularly during times of international instability. But weapons that risk catastrophic and irreversible humanitarian consequences cannot seriously be viewed as protecting civilians or humanity as a whole.

We know now more than ever before that the risks are too high, the dangers too real. It is time for States, and all those of us in a position to influence them, to act with urgency and determination to bring the era of nuclear weapons to an end.

* * *

In Hiroshima Peace Memorial Park

The heat of summer is oppressive.

Children pass by in groups, chattering.
They wear school outfits –
black pants or skirts and white shirts.

Some groups are wearing yellow caps.
They stop at Sadako's statue and,
in lilting voices, sing songs with words
I cannot understand.

When they finish their songs, they bow,
paying tribute to one of their own, Sadako,
forever young, a child of the bomb.

Though nearly seven decades have passed,
I feel guilty for what my country did here.

To whom can I apologize? To whom must
I apologize? It doesn't matter.
They have already forgiven, long ago.

David Krieger

Wake Up! *David Krieger's new poetry collection, published by the Nuclear Age Peace Foundation, $14.95 ISBN 978150098874 6*

At a First Aid Post

You
Who have no channels for tears when you weep
No lips through which words can issue when you howl
No skin for your fingers to grip with when you writhe in torment

You

Your squirming limbs all smeared with blood and slimy sweat and lymph
Between your closed lids the glaring eyeballs show only a thread of white
On your pale swollen bellies only the perished elastic that held up
  your drawers
You who can no longer feel shame at exposing your sheltered sex
O who could believe that
Only minutes ago
You were all schoolgirls fresh and appealing

In the scorched and raw Hiroshima
Out of dark shuddering flames
You no longer the human creatures you had been
Scrambled and crawled one after the other
Dragged yourselves along as far as this open ground
To bury in the dusts of agony
Your frizzled hair on skulls almost as bald as heads of Buddhist saints

Why should you have to suffer like this
Why suffer like this
What is the reason
What reason
And you
Do not know
How you look nor
What your humanity has been turned into

You are remembering
Simply remembering
Those who until this morning were
Your fathers mothers brothers sisters
(Would any of them recognise you now if they met you)

Remembering your homes where you used to sleep wake eat
(In a single flash all the flowers on their hedges were blasted
And no one knows where their ashes lie)
Remembering remembering
Here with your fellow-creatures who one by one gradually moving
Remembering
Those days when
You were daughters
Daughters of humankind

One of four Atomic Bomb poems by Toge Sankichi
Translated by James Kirkup
with help and advice from Fumiko Miura and Akiko Takemoto

' … It was this passion for oriental paintings that led me to visit, in London, the first exhibition of paintings devoted to the themes of atomic bomb horrors. They were by Iri Maruki and Toshiko Akamatsu, and were shown in Europe for the first time in 1955. These vividly realistic paintings made such a profound impression upon me that I went straight back to my room and wrote in longhand, at a single draft, the poem, 'Ghosts, Fire, Water' which I took straight back to the gallery, and laid it in the book of visitors' comments. Then I returned home and typed it out without any alterations and sent it to Kingsley Martin at *The New Statesman*, which had already published some of my work. It was rejected, without comment. By that time, I had received a response from the woman who had organised the exhibition, expressing her admiration and gratitude, and urging me to send it to British newspapers and periodicals. I sent out many copies but they were all either ignored or politely rejected. However, I managed to include it in my next volume of poems, *The Descent into the Cave* (Oxford University Press), two years later, in 1957. There were no reviews mentioning the poem.'

James Kirkup
Andorra, April 2004
No More Hiroshimas
Spokesman £6.99

Ghosts, Fire, Water

On the Hiroshima panels by Iri Maruki and Toshiko Akamatsu

These are the ghosts of the unwilling dead,
Grey ghosts of that imprinted flash of memory
Whose flaming and eternal instant haunts
The speechless dark with dread and anger.

Grey, out of pale nothingness their agony appears.
Like ash they are blown and blasted on the wind's
Vermilion breathlessness, like shapeless smoke
Their shapes are torn across the paper sky.

These scarred and ashen ghosts are quick
With pain's unutterable speech, their flame-cracked flesh
Writhes and is heavy as the worms, the bitter dirt;
Lonely as in death they bleed, naked as in birth.

They greet each other in a ghastly paradise,
These ghosts who cannot come with gifts and flowers.
Here they receive each other with disaster's common love,
Covering one another's pain with shrivelled hands.

They are not beautiful, yet beauty is in their truth.
There is no easy music in their silent screams,
No ordered dancing in their grief's distracted limbs.
Their shame is ours. We, too, are haunted by their fate.

In the shock of flame, their tears brand our flesh,
We twist in their furnace, and our scorching throats
Parch for the waters where the cool dead float.
We press our lips upon the river where they drink, and drown.

Their voices call to us, in pain and indignation:
'This is what you have done to us!'
Their accusation is our final hope. Be comforted.
Yes, we have heard you, ghosts of our indifference,

We hear your cry, we understand your warnings.
We, too, shall refuse to accept our fate!
Haunt us with the truth of our betrayal
Until the earth's united voices shout refusal, sing your peace!

Forgive us, that we had to see your passion to remember
What we must never again deny: *Love one another.*

James Kirkup
London, 1955

Detail from the Hiroshima Panels by Iri Maruki and Toshiko Akamatsu, whose work Kirkup saw in London in 1955.

Conversion of the heart

Nuclear zero lawsuits

David Krieger

David Krieger founded the Nuclear Age Peace Foundation in 1982. The Foundation, together with the International Association of Lawyers against Nuclear Arms (IALANA), sponsored a panel in Vienna in December 2014, for which this paper was prepared, in the days before the landmark international conference on the humanitarian impact of nuclear weapons at which 158 states participated as well as numerous international and civil society organisations.

The Nuclear Zero lawsuits, initiated by the Marshall Islands of the Pacific Ocean, are about the law, but they are about much more than the law. They are also about saving humanity from its most destructive capabilities. They are about saving humanity from itself and about preserving civilization for future generations. They are incredibly important, and I will try to place them in a broader context.

I will begin by sharing two quotations with you. The first is by Jayantha Dhanapala, a Sri Lankan diplomat, former United Nations Under-Secretary General, and long-time and committed leader in the area of nuclear disarmament. He states:

> 'The spectre of the use of a nuclear weapon through political intent, cyber-attack or by accident, by a nation state or by a non-state actor, is more real than we, in our cocoons of complacency, choose to acknowledge.'

The spectre of nuclear use, even nuclear war, is real and most of the world lives in 'cocoons of complacency'. It is clear that we must break free from those cocoons, which are as dangerous to the human future as are the nuclear weapons that now imperil us. The Nuclear Zero lawsuits seek to accomplish that.

The second quote is by His Holiness Pope Francis, the leader of the Catholic Church, who has brought new light and compassion to his office. He states:

> 'As long as so great a quantity of arms are in circulation as at present, new pretexts can always be found for initiating hostilities. For this reason, I make my own the appeal of my predecessors for the non-proliferation of arms and for disarmament of all parties, beginning with nuclear and chemical weapons disarmament.'

The Pope talks about disarmament in general, but he puts nuclear disarmament, along with chemical weapons disarmament, at the top of his list.

Pope Francis continues:

> 'We cannot however fail to observe that international agreements and national laws – while necessary and greatly to be desired – are not of themselves sufficient to protect humanity from the risk of armed conflict. A conversion of hearts is needed which would permit everyone to recognize in the other a brother or sister to care for, and to work together with, in building a fulfilling life for all.'

'A conversion of hearts.' Can there be any doubt that such conversion is necessary? Can there be any doubt that traditional diplomacy is not getting the job done? And that preparations for war and resolving conflicts by means of warfare are moving us farther away from the needed conversion of hearts?

Disarmament negotiations have been stuck for some 20 years. The 'step-by-step' approach of the nuclear-armed states is not working. There are no negotiations in good faith for nuclear disarmament, as required by international law. There are still over 16,000 nuclear weapons in the world. The use of even a small number of these would destroy civilization or, worse, end complex life on the planet – the only planet we know of in the universe that harbours life.

Nuclear weapons do not so much threaten our amazing planet itself, as they threaten the future of humanity and all the creatures, which are subject, for better or worse, to our stewardship. Over geological time, with the passing of hundreds of thousands of years, the Earth will recover from the worst we can do to it. It is ourselves and civilization that we put at risk with our nuclear arsenals. We must have a 'conversion of hearts' if we are to save our world, ourselves, and the human future.

The Marshall Islands has brought lawsuits against the nine nuclear-armed countries. They ask only that these nine nuclear-armed states do what is required of them under international law – under the Nuclear Non-Proliferation Treaty (NPT) and customary international law. They ask that the nuclear-armed countries fulfil their obligations under international law to pursue negotiations in good faith for an end to the nuclear arms race and for nuclear disarmament. They ask only for the fulfilment of unkept promises and unmet obligations.

The Marshall Islanders are very sympathetic heroes and heroines. For 12 years, from 1946 to 1958, the United States tested nuclear and thermonuclear weapons in the Marshall Islands, causing untold suffering to the islanders. The US tested 67 times, in the atmosphere and under water. The power of these tests was the equivalent force of testing 1.6 Hiroshima bombs daily for 12 years. This led to countless health problems and premature deaths from cancer and leukaemia. It also led to many birth defects and stillbirths. After the Japanese cities of Hiroshima and Nagasaki, no place on the planet has suffered more from nuclear weapons than have the Marshall Islands.

The United States was the trustee of the Trust Territory of the Pacific, which included the Marshall Islands. In this role, the US was responsible for protecting the life and health of the islanders. Instead, the US tested nuclear weapons on their islands, conducted secret radiation experiments on the islanders, and hid information from the islanders so as to evade paying them fair compensation for their pain, suffering and premature deaths. This was criminal behaviour; it was certainly not the behaviour of a responsible trustee.

With the Nuclear Zero lawsuits, the Marshall Islanders are acting out of compassion. They are not seeking compensation. They are breaking the bonds of complacency. They seek a conversion of the human heart in order to save their islands and the world from the ravages of nuclear weapons. They wish that no other country or people will ever suffer as they have. They have initiated these lawsuits as a public good.

As Marshall Islands Foreign Minister Tony de Brum put it,

> 'Our people have suffered the catastrophic and irreparable damage of these weapons, and we vow to fight so that no one else on earth will ever again experience these atrocities. The continued existence of nuclear weapons and the terrible risk they pose to the world threaten us all.'

I should note that this is the same perspective as that of the *hibakusha*, the survivors of Hiroshima and Nagasaki. It is the perspective of all those who have suffered the terrible consequences of nuclear weapons' use.

With regard to the legal aspects of these lawsuits, they are about whether treaties matter. They are about whether the most powerful nations are to be bound by the same rules as the rest of the international community. They are about whether a treaty can stand up with only half of the bargain fulfilled. They are about who gets to decide if treaty obligations are being met. Do all parties to a treaty stand on equal footing, or do the powerful have special rules specifically for them? They are also about the strength of customary international law to bind nations to civilized behaviour.

These lawsuits, as I already noted, are about more than just the law.

They are also about breaking the cocoons of complacency and a conversion of hearts. They are also about leadership, boldness, courage, justice, wisdom and, ultimately, about survival. Let me say a word about each of these.

Leadership. If the most powerful countries won't lead, then other countries must. The Marshall Islands, a small island country, has demonstrated this leadership, both on ending climate chaos and on eliminating the nuclear weapons threat to humanity.

Boldness. Many of us in civil society have been calling for boldness in relation to the failure of the nuclear-armed countries to fulfil their obligations to negotiate in good faith to end the nuclear arms race and to achieve complete nuclear disarmament. The status quo has become littered with broken promises, and these have become hard to tolerate. Instead of negotiating in good faith for an end to the nuclear arms race 'at an early date', the nuclear-armed countries have engaged in massive programmes of modernization of their nuclear arsenals (nuclear weapons, delivery systems and nuclear infrastructure). Such modernization of nuclear arsenals could cost trillions of dollars and ensure that nuclear weapons are deployed through the 21st century and beyond. The Marshall Islands is boldly challenging the status quo with the Nuclear Zero lawsuits.

Courage. The Marshall Islands is standing up for humanity in bringing these lawsuits. I see them as David standing against the nine nuclear-armed Goliaths. But the Marshall Islands is a David acting nonviolently, using the courts and the law instead of a slingshot. The Marshall Islands show us by their actions what courage looks like.

Justice. The law should always be about justice. In the case of nuclear weapons, both the law and justice call for an equal playing field, one in which no country has possession of nuclear weapons. That is the bargain of the Nuclear Non-Proliferation Treaty and the requirement of customary international law, and the Marshall Islands is taking legal action that seeks justice in the international community.

Wisdom. The lawsuits are about the wisdom to confront the hubris of the nuclear-armed countries. The arrogance of power is dangerous, and the arrogance of reliance upon nuclear weapons could be fatal for all humanity.

Survival. At their base, the Nuclear Zero lawsuits brought by the Marshall Islands are about survival. They are about making nuclear war, by design or accident, impossible because there are no longer nuclear weapons to threaten humanity. Without nuclear weapons in the world, there can be no nuclear war, no nuclear famine, no overriding threat to the human species and the future of humanity.

The dream of ending the nuclear weapons threat to humanity should be the dream not only of the Marshall Islanders, but also our dream as well, our collective dream, not only for ourselves, but also for the human future.

The people of the world should follow the lead of the Marshall Islanders. If they can lead, we can support them. If they can be bold, we can join them. If they can be courageous, we can be as well. If they can demand that international law be based on justice, we can stand with them. If they can act wisely and confront hubris, with all its false assumptions, we can join them in doing so. If they can take seriously the threat to human survival inherent in our most dangerous weapons, so can we. The Marshall Islands show us the way forward, breaking cocoons of complacency and demonstrating a conversion of the heart.

I am proud to be associated with the Marshall Islands and its extraordinary Foreign Minister, Tony de Brum. As a consultant to the Marshall Islands, the Nuclear Age Peace Foundation has worked to build the legal teams that support the Nuclear Zero lawsuits. We have also built a consortium of over 50 civil society organizations and individuals supporting the lawsuits. We have also created a way for individuals to add their voices of support with a brief petition. You can find out more and add your voice at the campaign website (address below).

I will conclude with a poem that I wrote recently:

Testing Nuclear Weapons in the Marshall Islands

The islands were alive
with the red-orange fire of sunset
splashed on a billowy sky.
The islanders lived simple lives
close to the edge of the ocean planet
reaching out to infinity.
The days were bright and the nights
calm in this happy archipelago
until the colonizers came.
These were sequentially the Spanish,
Germans, Japanese and then, worst of all,
the United States.
The US came as trustee
bearing its new bombs, eager to test them
in this beautiful barefoot Eden.
The islanders were trusting,

even when the bombs began exploding
and the white ash fell like snow.
The children played
in the ash as it floated down on them,
covering them in poison.
The rest is a tale of loss
and suffering by the islanders, of madness
by the people of the bomb.

www.nuclearzero.org
www.bmeia.gv.at

* * *

Our Common Home

Pope Francis told the Vienna Conference on the Humanitarian Impact of Nuclear Weapons:

'…Nuclear weapons are a global problem, affecting all nations, and impacting future generations and the planet that is our home. A global ethic is needed if we are to reduce the nuclear threat and work towards nuclear disarmament. Now, more than ever, technological, social and political interdependence urgently calls for an ethic of solidarity (cf. John Paul II, *Sollicitudo Rei Socialis*, 38), which encourages peoples to work together for a more secure world, and a future that is increasingly rooted in moral values and responsibility on a global scale.

The humanitarian consequences of nuclear weapons are predictable and planetary. While the focus is often placed on nuclear weapons' potential for mass-killing, more attention must be given to the 'unnecessary suffering' brought on by their use. Military codes and international law, among others, have long banned peoples from inflicting unnecessary suffering. If such suffering is banned in the waging of conventional war, then it should all the more be banned in nuclear conflict. There are those among us who are victims of these weapons; they warn us not to commit the same irreparable mistakes which have devastated populations and creation. I extend warm greetings to the *Hibakusha*, as well as other victims of nuclear weapons testing who are here at this meeting. I encourage them all to be prophetic voices, calling the human family to a deeper appreciation of beauty, love, co-operation and fraternity, while reminding the world of the risks of nuclear weapons which have the potential to destroy us and civilization.

Nuclear deterrence and the threat of mutually assured destruction cannot be the basis for an ethics of fraternity and peaceful coexistence among peoples and states. The youth of today and tomorrow deserve far more. They deserve a peaceful world order based on the unity of the human family, grounded on respect, co-operation, solidarity and compassion. Now is the time to counter the logic of fear with the ethic of responsibility, and so foster a climate of trust and sincere dialogue …

… In the context of this Conference, I wish to encourage sincere and open dialogue between parties internal to each nuclear state, between various nuclear states, and between nuclear states and non-nuclear states. This dialogue must be inclusive, involving international organisations, religious communities and civil society, and oriented towards the common good and not the protection of vested interests. 'A world without nuclear weapons' is a goal shared by all nations and echoed by world leaders, as well as the aspiration of millions of men and women. The future and the survival of the human family hinges on moving beyond this ideal and ensuring that it becomes a reality.

I am convinced that the desire for peace and fraternity planted deep in the human heart will bear fruit in concrete ways to ensure that nuclear weapons are banned once and for all, to the benefit of our common home … '

From the Vatican
7th December 2014

'Ken Coates was one of the very few people of pure genius and unbounded ambition I have known; yet wholly without ambition for himself, rather than a remarkable personal modesty. He possessed genius not only in imagination but also in delivery; such as conceiving the END appeal for European Nuclear Disarmament – wrongly attributed to Edward Thompson – on which he mobilised a broad range of actors in a truly Gramscian strategy of manoeuvre. Stressing also that this could be for a European nuclear free security zone, which influenced the Soviets in a manner that I have described in my recent book, *Europe in Question – and what to do about it,* which recounts also his key role in supporting alternative European strategies both before and after becoming a member of the European Parliament. These are only some of the reasons why it is vital that we should not only remember, but also still be inspired by him.'

Stuart Holland

Reparations Unpaid

Alexis Tsipras

The new Prime Minister of Greece spoke to the Inter-party Parliamentary Committee for Claiming German Reparations at its meeting at the Hellenic Parliament in Athens on 10 March 2015.

I take the floor today in this historic meeting not only for symbolic, but also for substantive reasons; first and foremost, to pay tribute to the victims of World War Two. But also to honour the male and female fighters from all over the world who gave their lives for the freedom of their homelands – who gave their lives in order to defeat Nazism, which threw its poisonous fog over the people of the world. I also take the floor to honour the fighters of the Greek national resistance, who gave their lives in order to rid the country of Nazi atrocities and occupation, in order for us to have a free, sovereign homeland today.

Some people say, 'Why tackle the past? Look to the future!' But how can a country, a people, have a future if it does not honour its history and its struggles? How can a people move forward, erasing collective memory and leaving its struggles and sacrifices historically unjustified?

Not much time has passed since then. The generation of the Occupation and of the National Resistance lives still. Echoes of torture and executions at Distomo and Kaisariani, at Kalavrita and at Vianno, are still fresh in the collective memory of our people. The crimes and destruction caused by the troops of the Third Reich across Greece, but also across the entirety of Europe, remain fresh in the memory of our people. And these memories must be preserved in the younger generations. We have a duty – historical, political, and ethical – to preserve them. Not because we want to retain the suspicion and hatred between peoples, but in order to remember forever what Nazism means, what fascism means. In order to remember that when solidarity, friendship, co-operation and dialogue between different people are replaced by a sense of superiority and historical destiny – when respect is supplanted by intolerance, both ethnic and social – then war and darkness prevail.

This darkness Europe has known well. It lived it, and hated it. This was one of the reasons why, in 1957, the European people decided to begin procedures so that the sirens of war would never sound again. We should not forget that the German people suffered, too, from Nazi atrocities; and that, in Germany, Nazism prevailed because the German people were humiliated at an earlier stage.

This, of course, is not an excuse but an explanation. It is the lesson of the short 20th century – if we remember Eric Hobsbawm well. After World War One, hatred and revanchism prevailed; there was short-sighted humiliation of the loser as punishment, the humiliation of an entire people, and misery visited upon them because of their defeat. And this choice was later paid in the blood of the youth of the entire world – including Germany's.

The people of Europe and their leaders must remember and draw conclusions from modern European history, because Europe must not be permitted to make the same mistakes again. After World War Two, the lesson was learned. Despite the crimes of the Third Reich and Hitler's hordes, who burned the world to the ground, despite the totalitarian evil of the Holocaust, Germany benefited, and rightfully so, from a series of interventions. The most important of these were the write-offs of Germany's debts, under the Agreement on German External Debts made in London in 1953 and, of course, the huge sums disbursed by the Allies in order to rebuild Germany.

The London Treaty recognises, however, that Germany's final reparations for World War Two remain. They should have been resolved at the time of the final peace agreement, which wasn't signed until 1990, due to the division of Germany. The reunification of the two Germanys created the necessary legal and political conditions to resolve this issue, but the German governments since then have opted for silence, legal tricks, deferment, and dilatory tactics. And I wonder, is this stance ethical?

I mentioned legal tricks, and since these are very important issues I would like to explain clearly what I mean, so that no shadow of a doubt remains. When Germany agrees to discuss its debts to Greece since World War Two, it invokes the Bilateral Agreement of 1960. This was when, by Germany's own initiative, it paid 115 million marks as reparations, and the then Kingdom of Greece acknowledged that there were no further claims to be had. This agreement, however, did not have to do with the reparations that involved the damages suffered by the country, but with the reparations to the victims of Nazism in Greece. And, of course, in no case whatsoever did it concern the Occupation Loan, or even the claims for reparations given the atrocities of war, the almost complete destruction of the infrastructure of the country, and the destruction of the economy during the war and the Occupation.

All these, I know well, are highly technical and highly sensitive issues, and perhaps this is not the place or the time to say more about them. The necessary clarifications and the technical work will not be done by me, but by experts – legal scholars and historians. I want to reassure both the Greek people and the German people that we will approach this issue with the necessary sensitivity, with a sense of responsibility and honesty, through communication and dialogue. But we expect the same thing from the German government, for reasons of a political, historical and symbolic nature.

In contrast to the moralising tone that has prevailed in the past few years within the public debate in Europe, we neither choose the position of the student who bends his head and closes his eyes against moral teaching from on high, nor do we choose the position of the moralising teacher, who wags his finger reproachfully at a supposed sinner, asking him to pay for his sins. On the contrary, we choose the path of negotiation and dialogue, of mutual understanding and justice. We will perform no theodicy here, but at the same time we will not give up our inalienable claims. We are not delivering lessons on morality; nor will we accept any morality lessons. Because, lately, when listening to provocative statements from abroad, I am often reminded of the famous passage from the Sermon on the Mount, when Jesus says: 'They see the mote in their brother's eye, but not the beam in their own'.

The Greek government will work tirelessly, on an equal footing and through dialogue in the framework of an honest negotiation, to find a solution to the most complex problems faced by Europe. The government will work to honour fully its obligations. But, at the same time, it will work to meet all the unfulfilled obligations owed to Greece and the Greek people. And in the same way that we commit to fulfil our own obligations, so the other sides ought to fulfil theirs, too. Morality cannot be invoked à la carte. It cannot happen by chance.

The new Greek government will support, with all its powers, the initiative to rebuild, reconstruct, and upgrade the Commission for Claiming the German Reparations to Greece. We will support it truly and substantively – not simply for show. We are ready to offer any political and legal assistance, so that the efforts of the Commission bear fruit; and in the framework of its tenure, to bring a meaningful result, to bring a solution, to vindicate the unfulfilled ethical, but also historical, debts, not only to the Greek people, but also to all of the peoples of Europe who fought and bled to defeat Nazism. We owe it to our history. We owe it to the fighters of the National Resistance in Greece. We owe it to the victims of World War Two. We owe it to Europe and its peoples, who have the right to a future unfettered by any kind of totalitarianism.

Our breath of life

Loula Vlahoutsikou-Giannakopoulou

In Athens in 1998, a conference was organised to present 'the historical, ethical and legal aspects of German war obligations to Greece'. Some years later, in 2012, the conference findings were incorporated in a new bilingual edition (Greek and English) of The Black Book of Occupation, *which recounts the 'Martyrology' of Greece at the hands of the Nazis.* Manolis Glezos MEP, *a hero of the Greek Resistance and one of Syriza's best known representatives, prepared the new text and presented a signed copy to The Spokesman in 2013, during a visit to the Hellenic Parliament of a delegation from the Greece Solidarity Campaign.*

Loula Vlahoutsikou-Giannakopoulou, *prisoner 42320, was in hospital at the time of the 1998 conference, and so she sent this written testimony. She had been a prisoner in the camps of Ravensbruck and Buchenwald, and was one of the 16 Greek women prisoners in the latter camp who survived.*

* * *

[…] I was standing with everyone else by the power lathe, at which we were forced to work by Nazis for 12 hours daily, grinding lethal cases for bullets. At some point, I was distracted and the roar of the lathe became the roar of the train, taking me back to my home, the isle of Evripos [Evia]. My imagination brought me back to my place, Limni, and my home. I was standing in the kitchen, by the window, looking at the pine needles coming in through the sieve and breathing the sweet smell of the pine. In the rhythm of the lathe I was hearing my mother's loom and her voice: 'Girls! Bring the coffee and the sour-cherry to your father!'

It was a summer afternoon. In this very place our father would sit down after his siesta to smell the pine fragrance, while sipping his coffee. The faces of my family passed before my eyes. I kept them in my mind as a talisman, and brought them out at the most critical moments. I thought of their hands, wondering on which hand my father wore his stone ring, which a few years ago I was twiddling in my finger, playing …

My mother, I remember, wore her wedding ring on her middle finger. Would I ever wear a wedding ring?

Suddenly, a case flew by my ear, thrown with hate by the Nazi supervisor. It seems that she felt number 42320 had escaped hell for a few minutes and had committed the crime of becoming a human being again, a dreaming girl. No! For her I had to remain number 42320 until death. Nothing else …

I exchanged glances with my compatriots. We talked with our eyes. We were in pain, hungry, freezing cold, in the fire of fever, but we kept working. We used only our eyes to talk to each other.

Without making clumsy gestures, to keep the supervisor from suspecting anything, I bent down over the box where the cartridge cases fell, and started mixing them up; you see, we used to put a small piece of iron in the lathe which produced a cut in the cases, making them defective for their deadly purpose. This organised sabotage from all of us prisoners was our revenge, our breath of life, our pride. The supervisor moved away while I continued mixing the defective cases. I felt our youth resistance song welling from deep inside me.

Even from this wretched rampart, we kept on the fight of our people, the fight of our generation.

Insubordinate! Human beings! Not numbers …

Gifts from Greece?

Frances O'Grady

Prior to Syriza's substantial victory in Greece's General Election of 25 January 2015, the General Secretary of the Trade Union Congress in Britain spelt out some of its wider issues for people across Europe. Later, when the new Greek government had been elected with a strong mandate to reverse austerity, the TUC General Council developed its message of solidarity.

This Sunday, the Greek people go to the polls in what must be one of the most important elections not just for Greece but for Europe as a whole. What is at stake is the future of democratic control of the economy, and the European establishment's love affair with austerity.

Nowhere in Europe has suffered so much from the after-effects of the global financial crisis. The austerity programme imposed on the Greek people by the troika of the IMF, the European Central Bank and the European Commission has seen unemployment rocket to 25% (and more than 50% among young people), the minimum wage and pensions slashed, public services sold off and in some cases – for example, Greece's public service broadcaster – shut down. Many Greek people have been left destitute, homeless and fearing for their futures. Some have left the country or abandoned their hopes of starting a family.

Above all, these changes have undermined democratic control in the country known as the birthplace of democracy – something that has helped the neo-nazi thugs of Golden Dawn grow. Unelected forces from outside the country have dictated the terms on which the Greek government and economy can continue to function. Labour's equivalent in Greece, PASOK, has all but collapsed under the strain. Collective bargaining has been undermined, and the unions' role reduced to fire-fighting, resisting closures, sell-offs and attacks on living standards.

For the rest of us in Europe, the elections are important because they could see the rejection of austerity and renewed discussion of the sort of sustainable investment plans that the ETUC has advocated. The IMF has – astoundingly, without showing any remorse – accepted that the levels of austerity they helped impose on Greece were based on flawed economic models. Every serious commentator I know acknowledges that, somehow, Greece's debt needs to be reduced, and that continued austerity in Greece is not the answer. That means some form of rescheduling the debt, including debt forgiveness, must be arranged, and the infamous Memorandum, under which Greek national sovereignty and economic sustainability were removed, needs to be replaced.

The costs of the global economic crisis need to be shared more fairly and, of course, there are problems in Greece that exacerbated the crisis, and are not externally imposed. Public debt was too high before the crisis. But that wasn't the fault of the people who are now paying for austerity: Greece needs to address the oligarchy that led it down the ruinous path it was already following before the global financial crisis hit, and whose members have so far not had to pay the price.

Although the Greek people have suffered most under austerity, if they reject it that will have repercussions in forthcoming elections across Europe – starting with Spain – because austerity is hitting everyone (arguably, it already hit Germany in the last decade when pay growth stagnated and the sort of low paid jobs we are used to in the UK spread to Europe's richest economy.) The UK's working poor and middle classes have also suffered from the ideological craze for slashing the state back to the size it was in the 1930s, the spread of low-productivity and zero hours jobs, and stagnating wages.

Now every poll shows Syriza, the left party headed by Alexis Tsipras, who I met last year, in the lead. Some European politicians have, disgracefully, been threatening the Greek elctorate with dire consequences, including expulsion from the Eurozone, if they dare to vote the wrong way! There are powerful forces mobilising against the interests of the Greek people. So if they choose an alternative path on Sunday, they will deserve and need our support and solidarity.

* * *

Solidarity with Greek Workers

Following Syriza's substantial general election victory on 25 January 2015, the TUC General Council issued this statement.

The TUC General Council, representing 6 million trade unionists in Britain, sends greetings and solidarity to the people and trade unions of

Greece, through our sister organisations ADEDY and GSEE.

Greek workers and their families and communities have suffered terribly in the five years since the financial crisis began, and in particular since the troika – the European Commission, European Central Bank and the IMF – imposed the infamous Memorandum on the Greek people. Austerity and structural reforms have shrunk the economy by a quarter, produced unemployment of over 25% (over 50% for young people) and seen public services slashed or even closed down as is the case with the public service broadcaster ERB. Minimum wages and pensions have been cut, collective bargaining rights and a voice for workers on the economy have been destroyed, and lives have been ruined: even suicide rates have risen dramatically. The TUC expressed its concern and solidarity with Greek workers and their unions in a resolution at Congress in 2013 and we have since worked closely with the Greece Solidarity Campaign – our support for which we reiterate - and our sister organisations in Greece.

These measures have not been confined to Greece – they are part of a global assault on workers and ordinary people which has led to increasing inequality, falling living standards for the majority and any gains from growth going to the already rich and powerful. Across Europe, workers' rights are under attack and living standards have fallen or been frozen. Deflation – in part due to lack of wages-driven demand and in some countries excessive personal debt - is now the biggest risk facing the European economies.

The election of the Syriza-led government in Greece in January has therefore given hope not only to the Greek people but to people across Europe. It has already signalled its commitment to meet union demands big and small, such as restoring the value of minimum wages and pensions, pro-poor social policies, reopening the ERB public service broadcaster, re-employing the striking cleaners at the Finance Ministry and ceasing the privatisation of Piraeus port, as well as giving Greek-born children of migrants citizenship rights. Prime Minister Alexis Tsipras has gone on record pledging 'to end the medieval regulation of the labour market created by the troika to serve the interests of the oligarchs', meaning the restoration of collective wage bargaining. The TUC welcomes these moves.

We urge the international community – and especially European institutions and governments – to give Greece room to breathe economically. As ETUC General Secretary Bernadette Segol has said: 'Greece's debt burden is unbearable and must be relieved. European Union policies have created a disaster'. In particular, we call on those governments currently resisting the negotiation of a fair deal on Greek debt to consider the hardship imposed by the Memorandum, and the likely beneficiaries of any further moves to over-ride the democratic will of the Greek people, including the neo-nazis in Golden Dawn who pose a threat to social cohesion and trade unionism.

We urge progressive politicians across the EU to learn the lesson that it is the role of democratically elected governments to protect workers' fundamental human rights and people's living standards from market forces rather than the other way around. And we call on trade unionists in the UK and across Europe to show solidarity with the Greek workers and unions in defending the Greek government's programme of social justice and redistribution, and its programme of genuine structural reform to tackle the power of the oligarchs.

* * *

Wishful

A post-Millennial noon. Greek priest let down the metal pail,
cranking it back with slow, deliberate turns to greet
politely these half-dozen Western travellers –
a mild, sceptical bunch, no pilgrims, but all linked
by growing disbelief and shared distaste for politics.
Weighing up myths, we marvelled that a Christian church
could suavely welcome walkers and boast of renovation
on a lavish scale while nearby at Nablus
a myriad refugees crammed into Balata camp.

A mortal right's too often claimed; the stern religionist
may terrorize and kill, evict and dispossess the natives:
such seems the fate of Palestine – the Promised Land, say thieves,
those Zionists and zealous settlers who impose
their own apartheid on the mainly Muslim *Untermensch*.
What deity exists, empowered to promise anything?
Context is all, not blinkered folly; calmer vision's missed,
as are new angles. One might wish for some cool insight gained
through thinking clear and drinking deep from Jacob's Well.

Alexis Lykiard

photo Gerry Murray

Jonathan Pryce as Gethin Price
at the Nottingham Playhouse, 1975

Comedians

Trevor Griffiths

We asked Trevor Griffiths to suggest an excerpt from his acclaimed play to mark the 40th anniversary of Comedians' *first production at Nottingham Playhouse, on 20 February 1975, directed by Richard Eyre. He chose this scene at the end of Act Two, which begins with detailed stage directions.*

Price emerges, carrying the tiny violin and bow. He wears bagging half-mast trousers, large sullen boots, a red hard wool jersey, studded and battered denim jacket, sleeves rolled to elbows, a red and white scarf tied on to an arm. His face has been subtly whitened to deaden and mask the face. He is half clown, half this year's version of bovver boy. The effect is calculatedly eerie, funny and chill. He takes out a deeply filthy handkerchief, spreads it carefully, expertly across his right shoulder, slowly tucks the tiny violin on his left, stands perfectly still, looks for the first time at the audience. Cocks the bow, stares at it intently, apparently sinking into process. Notices a very fine thread of gut hanging down. Shakes the bow. Shakes it again. The thread hangs on. He brings the bow finally to his mouth, tries to bite the thread off, his teeth are set on edge, he winces mutely, tries again, can't. He thinks. Tries, bending oddly on one leg, to trap the thread under his huge boot. Fails. Thinks. Takes out a lighter. Sets fire to the thread. Satisfaction. Makes as if to play. The cocked bow slowly begins to smoulder at the far end. He waves it about, horrified. The violin now begins to play unaided in his other hand a piece of intricate Bach. He's trapped for a moment between the two events; finally he places the spent bow on the stage, puts the violin under his boot, dimps it like a cigarette until it's thoroughly crushed.

PRICE *(to himself, not admitting the audience's existence)* Wish I had a train. I feel like smashing a train up. On me own. I feel really strong. Wish I had a train. I could do with some exercise.

He does a complicated kata, with praying mantis footsweeps, a tan-fui, pa-kua dao, and other kung fu exercises. A spot suddenly illuminates larger than life-size dummies of a youngish man and woman carried on by a club-hand. Well dressed, beautiful people, a faint unselfconscious arrogance in their carriage. The man wears evening dress, gloves, etc., the girl, a simple, stunning white full-length dress and wrap. Her arm is looped in his. They stand, perhaps waiting for a cab to show after the theatre. Price has continued his exercises throughout this 'arrival'. Becomes aware of them gradually: rises slowly: stares. Turns to the audience, slowly smiles, evil and childlike. Sniffs. Ambles over. Stands by the man, measuring, walks round to stand by the girl. We sense him being ignored. He begins to inspect the girl minutely. Takes a cigarette from pocket.

Cigarette? *(Nothing. He offers it to the man.)* No? *(He pockets the cigarette, turns, calls 'Taxi!' sharply out front, shakes his head as it disappears. Moves round to the man's side again.)* Are you the interpreter, then? Been to the match, have we? Were you at t'top end wi' lads? Good, wannit? D'you see Macari? Eh? *(Silence.)* P'raps I'm not here. Don't you like me? You hardly know me. Let's go and have a pint, get to know each other. Here, don't you live in Salford? I swear I've seen you at the dog track. *(Nothing. He takes a cigarette out of the man's top pocket.)* Very kind of you. Ta. *(He lights the cigarette, blows the smoke in slow separate puffs across the man's face.)* Int this nice? I like a good chat. *(intimate, man-to-man)* Eh. I bet she's a goer, int she, sunshine? She's got a fair pair of knockers on her too. Has she been around? Does she ever go dancing at Belle Vue, Satdays? I think Eric Yates took her home one night. If it's her, she's a right goer, according to Eric. *(Pause.)* I don't know whether to thump you one or what. I suppose I could just give you a clout, just to let you know I exist. *(He blows smoke into the man's face.)* Is that hair dyed? Looks dyed. Are you a puff? Are you a pufter? *(Sniffs. Front, fast) Taxi! (Pause.)* That's not a taxi, lady, it's a hearse. *(Evilish grin)* You're getting confused, lady. Unless you were thinking of a quick fun funeral before retiring for the night. *(to man)* Say something, Alice? She's calling hearses, he's talking to himself. *(He turns back to the man.)* You do speak, do you? I'm trying to talk to you. Say some'at. Tell us what kind of day you've had. Are you on the buses? Eh. Shall I make you laugh? This feller pays twenty pounds for this whore, right? Only she dunt fancy him and runs out of the room. He chases her, stark nekkid, down t'street. Cop stops him, says, Where's the fire, lad? Feller says, I've no idea, but if you see a nude bird running down street, fuck her, it's paid for. *(Pause. Nothing.)*You can laugh, you know, I don't mind you laughing. I'm talking to you … There's people'd call this envy, you know, it's not, it's hate. *(Now very fast)* Are you a bi-sexual or is that your sister? You'll never get a taxi here, they're all up at Piccadilly waiting for t'last train from London. Ask me how I know. I work there that's why. And don't interrupt when I'm talking, dint your mother ever tell you, it's rude? *(He does a kung fu thrust, missing the man's head by inches.)* Bruce Lee, do you like him? God, he is. You're a stuck-up bastard, aren't you? Give me a kiss, then, go on Alice, give us a kiss. I love you, give us a kiss. *(He halts his burble. Blinks. Pads round to stand at woman's side.)* Say something? *(In her ear)* Listen… I've got a British Rail delivery truck round the corner, ditch Alice and we'll do the town. *(He notices a folded copy of* The Times *in the man's hand. Passes behind the figures, pops his head between them.)* Crosswords? *(Thinks a moment.)* Election. Nine across. Big poll in China, question mark. *(Chinaman)* E-lection, *(Price looks from one to the other, laughs suddenly. He takes hold of their handles, begins to lift them up and down, to indicate their mirth.)* Election! Election! Big poll in China. Laugh, you buggers, laugh! *(Price exhorts them to laugh, squeezing their bodies up and down and voicing their laughter for them. Then, very suddenly)* Here. *(He takes a flower out of his pocket, offers it to them.)* For the lady. No, no, I have a pin. *(Pause. He pins the flower – a marigold – with the greatest delicacy between the girl's breasts. Steps back to look at his work.)* No need for thanks, my pleasure entirely. Believe me.

Silence. Nothing. Then, a dark red stain, gradually widening, begins to form behind the flower.

Aagh, aagh, aagh, aagh …

The spot shrinks slowly on the dummies, centring finally on the red stain. Price's 'aaghs' become short barks of laughter. Innocence.

I wonder what happened. P'raps it pierced a vein.

Their light goes out altogether. We're left with his single chill image.

I made them laugh, though. *(depressed)* Who needs them? Hunh. Who needs them? We manage. *(chanting)* U-n-i-ted.Uni-ted. You won't keep us down there for long, don't worry. We're coming up there where we can gerrat yer *(Chants.)* Lou Macari, Lou Macari … I shoulda smashed him one. They allus mek you feel sorry for 'em, out in the open. I suppose I shoulda just kicked him without looking at him. *(Pause. He looks after them. Calling)* National Unity? Up yours, sunshine. *(Pause. He picks up a tiny violin, i.e. another, switched, uncrushed, and a bow. Addresses it. Plays 'The Red Flag' – very simple and direct.)* Still, I made the buggers laugh …

Price walks off. The Concert Secretary, probably shocked, embarrassed, not wishing to dwell. Lights fade. Waters stands, face gaunt, grey. Challenor tosses down a scotch, sheafs his notes, pockets pen.

CONCERT SECRETARY: That's the lot, ladies and gentlemen. You have your cards, I think. Charlie Shaw has 'em for them that hasn't, and we're starting right away, settle yourselves down, now. And it's eyes down for a full house …

Lights fades gradually.

Always look after … Number One.

Lights fade to black.

* * *

Comedians *is published in Volume I of* Theatre Plays *by Trevor Griffiths, the first of two volumes which include 15 plays in all (Spokesman, £15 each).*

'Something as ugly as this joke'

Stanton B Garner Jr

Professor Garner teaches at the University of Tennessee.

More than any other play he has written, *Comedians* has identified Griffiths in the popular, theatrical and academic imagination. From its opening at the Nottingham Playhouse on 20 February 1975 (under the direction of Richard Eyre) to its subsequent opening in London at the Old Vic (24 September) and in the West End (Wyndham's Theatre, 27 January 1976), *Comedians* was widely acclaimed in the popular press. It soon became the work by which most North Americans were introduced to Griffiths as a writer. A production directed by Mike Nichols opened on Broadway at the Music Box Theater on 28 November 1976, and, although this particular production received mixed reviews, it was widely considered one of the season's most significant plays. Jonathan Pryce, a previously unknown actor who had originated the role of Gethin Price in Nottingham, earned a Tony Award for his performance, and a film version of the play was briefly considered (Griffiths's television adaptation of the play was broadcast as part of BBC's *Play for Today* series on 25 October 1979). The play has been revived a number of times – a highly acclaimed 1993 revival of the play by the West Yorkshire Playhouse moved that summer to the Lyric Theatre, Hammersmith – and it has been performed in translation around the world: *L'école des comiques* was performed by Le Théâtre National de Belgique in May 1976, *Komiker* was produced in Hamburg in January 1978, and the played has subsequently been staged as far away as Shanghai. In March 1987 *Comedians* was presented by an all-woman cast at the Everyman Theatre in Liverpool;

in April 1992 it was performed at the Court Theater in Chicago by an all-black and Hispanic cast in a production directed by Barney Simon of the Johannesburg Market Theatre. Griffiths adapted the play for both productions (Chicago comedian Aaron Freeman helped him with the latter adaptation). The play's influence has extended beyond the theatre: until it was withdrawn in 1993, *Comedians* was on the Associated Examining Board A-level exam list, and Griffiths accepted a dozen or so invitations a year to discuss the play with students and teachers.

It is easy to see why *Comedians* received such widespread popular interest. 'I wanted it to be like some of my television plays,' Griffiths has commented, 'more immediately accessible to people who haven't had a background in revolutionary theory or revolutionary history or whatever'. Shifting terrain from the history of socialist struggle and the Left's internal debates, Griffiths chose a topic more fully grounded in interpersonal interactions and hence (as the play's amenability to cultural translation suggests) more generalisable. At the same time, while *Comedians* may not be 'overtly' marked by revolutionary theory (given the scarcity of socialist writings on the topic of humour, this isn't surprising), its concerns and techniques draw upon the central preoccupations of Griffith's work as a whole. Indeed, part of the play's achievement is its demonstration that comedy and laughter constitute sites of often intricate political and ethical negotiation. Laughter, for Griffiths, is a social act that is caught up in questions of inclusion and exclusion, liberation and entrapment, involvement and distance. Griffiths explores the politics of this ostensibly apolitical field while using the devices of comedic performance to engage his audience with unusual directness. Through a series of reflexive gestures *Comedians* asks us to think about its own dramaturgical foundations, raising questions about performativity (comic and otherwise) while exploring the instabilities and interfaces of realism as a political aesthetic.

The idea for *Comedians* came to Griffiths in a Manchester bar, where he fell into conversation with a couple of stand-up comedians who had been taping sessions for a Granada TV series entitled *The Comedians* (this popular show, which ran between 1971and 1985, featured stand-up comics delivering jokes from the workingmen's club circuit to a studio audience). These comedians mentioned an older comedian, veteran of the local club circuit, who ran a class for local comics upstairs in a pub. Griffiths, who had been fascinated by stand-up comics since he first encountered them in local halls during the late 1940s and early 1950s, was drawn to this anecdote. In addition to the question of what it took to be a stand-up comic (and how someone would go about teaching a skill that seems so instinctual), the anecdote underscored a contradiction within the profession as a whole. While the comedians spoke of this teacher as someone whose practice was grounded in principle, their own careers were based on jokes that pandered to the audience's basest prejudices. Griffiths found himself reflecting upon the tradition of stand-up comedy and the contrasts between the antagonistic stance of much contemporary comedy and the tradition's earlier roots in a music-hall, working-class culture, in which comedy (in the hands of comedians like Frank Randle) was used to confront and come to terms with shared concerns. These reflections were also personal, for the issue of comedy foregrounded for Griffiths his own involvement in the contradictions he encountered:

> 'What none of us really explores inside the liberal cultural tradition is contradiction. And the contradiction that increasingly preoccupied me was: "Why do I laugh until my frame shakes at something as ugly as this joke?" '

* * *

Extract from Trevor Griffiths: Politics, Drama, History *by Stanton B Garner Jr., University of Michigan Press, 1999*

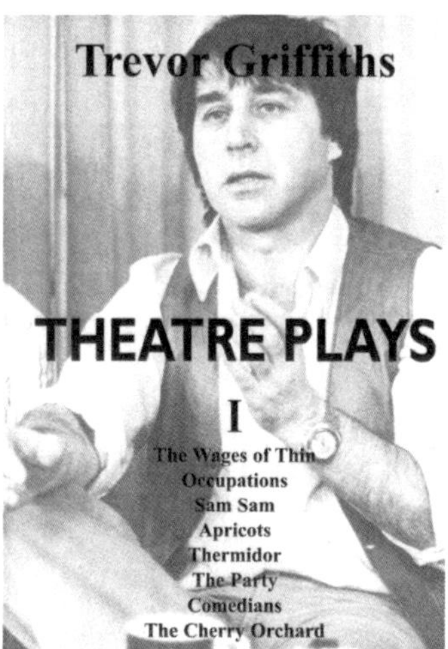

- AFTER WILLIAM BLAKE -
serco
NHS, thou art sick.
The invisible worms
that fly in the night
In the howling storm
Have found out thy bed
Of caring joy
And their dark
secret love
Does thy life
destroy.
care UK
HCA
BMI
Spire Healthc
NHS
©Steve Bell 2015 · 3763 · 7 · 1 ·

Save our NHS

Benedict Cooper
Zenn Athar
Ursula Holdsworth

Nottingham is on the frontline of some of the most radical and severely damaging changes to the NHS since its creation in the 1940s. Local activists, under the banner of 'The Nottingham We Deserve', investigate.

When five of the UK's leading dermatologists quit the Queen's Medical Centre in December 2014, Nottingham was thrust into the middle of a gathering storm of political debate. To many their departure was the latest symbol of a health service breaking down, and a workforce under increasing pressure. The doctors wouldn't be drawn on the issue, but sources quoted deep discomfort about a big decision that had quietly happened away from the public's eye: the unit was to be run by Circle, a private company.

Unite the Union's head of health, Rachael Maskell, says the case in Nottingham was a key moment for many campaigning against the growing influence of private healthcare companies such as Circle in the service. 'It showed the strength of feeling people have towards the NHS,' she says. 'It's not just an ideological step they took, it's also a clinical point of view. The consultants were willing to forfeit their careers to protect care in Nottingham.'

So why is there such strength of feeling? And what made the doctors quit? As activists in Nottingham and further afield know, the QMC case is just the tip of the iceberg. Everywhere you go, services are being taken over by private companies operating under the NHS logo; big business is moving in. This is nothing particularly new, but one thing alone has caused a major acceleration of the takeover of NHS services by profit driven companies. In 2012, the government passed a major piece of legislation, the Health and Social Care Act. Somewhere buried deep within this long and involved document was an innocuous sounding but incendiary new rule: NHS trusts would be required to go through competitive tendering for all new contracts. In short, NHS trusts would be forced to pay private companies to run their services, and pay for the administration of the whole bidding process – with taxpayer money.

Within this new rule lies the root of the Queen's Medical Centre's dermatology row, and dozens more like it up and down the country. Private companies are picking up NHS contracts, paid for by taxpayer money, with one thing in mind: turning a profit. And how do they do this? By treating the whole thing as a business; by taking aim at the lucrative contracts and leaving the risky ones well alone; by slashing staffing costs through staff redundancies, leaving the rest on cheaper, often zero-hour contracts.

It's a whole new business culture in health that former QMC psychiatrist, Dr Arun Chopra, speaking in January 2015, claims is slowly eroding services.

> 'So much time goes into creating business models now,' he said. 'We're seeing services competing with each other, services pitted against each other. I'm spending more and more time and tax-payer money dealing with bureaucracy; it's not what I wanted to do.'

This is a growing trend, which Ben Clements, a community mental health nurse in Nottingham and member of campaign group Keep Our NHS Public (KONP), says is having a direct effect on services and working conditions in the city:

> 'Already our NHS mental health beds are being reduced, and private companies are stepping in to fill the inevitable gap. It's not a business, it never has been; it's a public service, and we shouldn't forget the unique values that brings. People don't want the glossy brochures and the spin. They don't want lawyers fighting over contracts for who does what. They want decent care.'

In Nottingham there has been a spate of alarming changes to care, not least the planned closure of two mental health wards at Queen's Medical Centre. And when the crisis in A&E services in England first became apparent, back in January, Nottingham was sadly back in the news once again. GP and NHS campaigner Dr Bob Gill says this could well continue as more contracts go to companies such as private equity-owned Circle – which itself hit the news in January 2015 when it walked away from a whole hospital contract, unable to turn a profit. He says:

> 'The NHS is being turned into a corporate structure modelled on the private sector, in Nottingham and across the country. A&E is not profitable, it's very high risk. A&E units are being shut across the country to focus on the profitable services.'

* * *

Keep our NHS public

Ursula Holdsworth is a retired community paediatrician and member of Keep Our NHS Public (KONP).

'I got involved back in 2011,' she says. 'I could see what was beginning to happen to the NHS and the changes that were coming in under the Coalition. I could see it was going to be a hugely expensive reorganisation and a tremendous waste of £3bn.'

Ursula joined the Nottingham branch of national organisation Keep Our NHS Public in 2011, since when she has been active on the campaigning scene, speaking at public meetings and raising awareness of the changes to the NHS. The group organises regular meetings, public stalls and demonstrations, often linking up with unions and other campaign groups and taking part in wider, local, regional and national rallies.

As a career-long NHS doctor Ursula says that the rise of private companies in the NHS has spelled bad news for patient care, and for loyal staff: 'Private companies are just in it for a quick buck; they don't care what happens to a hospital long term. They see the NHS budget as an enormous opportunity.'

One of the most contentious local issues has been Circle's running of the Treatment Centre at QMC, and this, says Ursula, has been a big driver of her own campaigning. 'I knew that when it first opened all the staff there were NHS staff with NHS terms and conditions. Gradually they left and were replaced, and gradually the terms and conditions have been getting worse, and staff are no longer in the NHS pension.'

* * *

The Nottingham We Deserve is a campaign by the People's Assembly and Unite Community to tell the story of the cuts in our city and how they affect us. We know austerity has created food bank Britain, but do we hear the stories of the users of food banks or those made homeless by the financial crash? These articles are from The Nottingham We Deserve's newspaper.

www.nottinghamwedeserve.org

I Love This Body

Caroline Salzedo

I love this body: the body that I know. It anchors me; takes me away from the chattering 'monkey mind'. When I breathe, the monkey quietens. My lungs expand and massage the heart housed between them.

In Chinese Medicine, the heart is the Emperor and good health occurs when the Emperor is happy. How often has my Emperor been happy? I send her my focus as if I am holding a delicate, precious baby.

Is it her who sends these butterflies into my stomach? They release an aching that I cannot name, dark like a thicket of thorns. I ease my fingers underneath the ribs deep into the tissue. Gentle tears bubble up. Then with my slow, measured breathing, my stomach feels caressed; the tears stop; the butterflies still. Perhaps they have become dragonflies floating on the now-calm sea of my stomach.

The aching thicket is softening: it has been a lifetime's work to create; it is a lifetime's work to unravel.

From my stomach, liquid spurts through a valve into the small intestine. The pulsing rhythm of peristalsis is like a spiral, like the tides of the sea and movements of the universe. One of my Shiatsu teachers says it comes from your mother's egg at conception, at that alchemical moment when something new is created. I send my mind back to the spring when it happened. Perhaps birds sang like they do now.

The small intestine is deep in the body, not attached to the abdominal wall; a long thin tube with inner projections like sea anemones. Textbooks say the surface area is the size of a tennis court. It reverberates to change. In Chinese Medicine, it sorts the pure from the impure. As children, it's our

Caroline Salzedo describes herself as a 'Shiatsu practitioner and teacher, writer, wanderer and crone'. Some of her stories are based on time spent in revolutionary Nicaragua during the 1980s.

'I Love this Body' is from A Sense of Place*, a collection of work published in 2015 by Nottingham Writers' Studio to mark the group's arrival in new premises in Hockley, one of the city's old thoroughfares.*

parents' role to do that, and protect us from shock. If they don't, as I know from all the small intestines I have massaged and tended like gardens, a deep need develops in the cells for safety and shelter. I breathe, for all the times when I felt lost and unsafe as a child. Now only I can make it better.

The whole sea of the digestive system is calmer. Peristalsis is like a stately minuet. I take my focus to the valve between the small and large intestines, down by the appendix, where it changes from a narrower tube to a wider one; from taking things in to letting them go: a pivotal place. I feel a whirring, like it is out of kilter, and I rub it, see it in my mind's eye opening easily, without spluttering.

Up the ascending colon, across and down the descending colon. The pillars of the large intestine whose strength holds us up are like one long tube on either side of our body. I imagine them filled with golden liquid, suffused with sunlight.

I breathe and take my hand round the right side to say hello to my liver; vital to life. What a name! The liver has a spark like the flash of inspiration. I feel it can take me anywhere in the universe: a magic carpet; my bottle with a genie and all the wishes in the world, if I but know how to ask.

And then the back; my spine and kidneys: my life story, told without pretence or bluster. We can put on a front. We cannot put on a back. Everything lies hidden here. The place between my shoulder blades where I erected walls behind my heart, and my back erupted with pain. Stories going right back to being alone in the darkness of the womb. In my mind's eye, I have held that delicate, precious baby, like I held my heart, and sent her love.

Breathe; remember that the stories are no more. They are in the past. I am sitting in a room in a familiar house. Outside, birds are singing. Reality is this body I love and know.

My hands take me to a place of healing where I acknowledge the fear and joy of everything known and unknown. My breath unfolds and ripples, and something opens like a trap door, connecting me out into the universe and down into my deepest cells.

* * *

Nottingham Writers' Studio supports the development of creative writing in all its forms around the City. Currently, Nottingham seeks recognition by the United Nations Educational, Scientific, and Cultural Organization (Unesco) as a City of Literature.

Conscientious Objection

Jo Vellacott

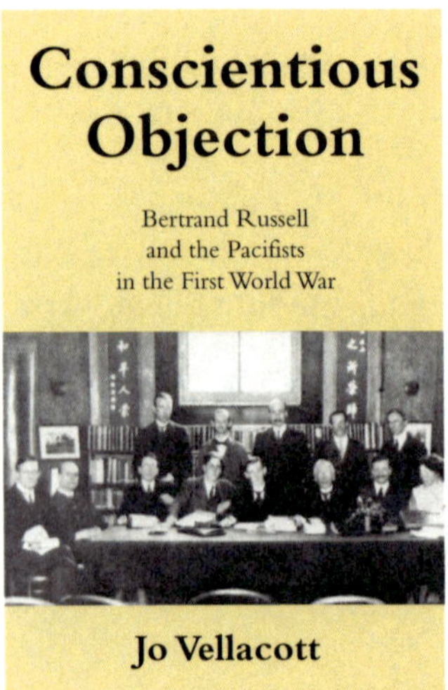

Jo Vellacott is a doyenne among peace historians, whose pioneering work will inform a new generation of peace activists. Resident in Canada for many years, she spent her formative years in England. In 1969, she discovered the unsorted papers of Catherine Marshall in the Cumbria Record Office and saw that they were full of previously unknown material about Bertrand Russell's work with conscientious objectors. These papers had been rescued but no funds were available to catalogue them, so Jo undertook this mammoth labour of love, sorting the First World War materials useful for her own research and then finishing the rest, which covered Marshall's activities for suffrage and then for the Women's International League for Peace and Freedom. Jo's acclaimed book, Bertrand Russell and the Pacifists in the First World War, *was first published in 1980. In 2015, Spokesman is republishing it under the title* Conscientious Objection. *Her introduction to this new edition, reprinted here, explains how she came to focus on the thousands of conscientious objectors. Jo's review article of Cyril Pearce's important book,* Comrades in Conscience, *follows.*

* * *

The 1960s and 1970s brought a revived interest in opposition to war and in ways of working for peace; also, largely through his visibility in the anti-nuclear weapons movement, in the peace work of Bertrand Russell. Now, four decades later, many of us are again, and urgently, beginning to tire of the study of war and to look back at previous opposition to war and forward to further work on alternatives. We should be considering how to do away with it altogether.

Meanwhile, the centenary of the First World War has come round, bringing with it an important opportunity to make sure that those who resisted war fever, refusing to be part of the killing, be remembered for their wisdom and courage alongside those whom we remember for their courage and, alas, for their obedience to the demands of authority. It is some time since I was engaged in active research, although I am still writing, and I am seeking ways to put to use my reservoir of knowledge of those who refused to fight in the war, and those who dedicated themselves to helping them resist.

I am glad to have this book become available again, virtually unchanged, but with a new title to emphasise the role of the Conscientious Objectors. Although this story of the No-Conscription Fellowship (NCF) focuses on Bertrand Russell's contribution, it has been recognised as contributing to an understanding of how the NCF was made up, how it worked, its successes and failures, and dissensions within it, particularly over the acceptability of various forms of alternative service and of political action in the cause of peace. On the Russell shelf, it pairs neatly with Nicholas Griffin's new *A Pacifist at War* (Spokesman, 2014) which, through a selection of letters, gives a vivid picture of Russell's complicated personal life, the background to his work in the cause of peace. On the history shelf its companions include, among others, Thomas Kennedy's *The Hound of Conscience* (University of Arkansas, 1981); David Boulton's *Objection Overruled* (new edition, Dales Historical Monographs, 2014); John Rae's *Conscience and Politics* (Oxford University Press, 1970); for women's work for peace, Sybil Oldfield's *Thinking Against the Current* (Sussex Academic Press, 1913; reviewed in *Spokesman 127* by Jo Vellacott); and, for a more general overview of opposition to the First World War, Adam Hochschild's *To End All Wars* (Houghton Mifflin, 2011). Other essential work on conscientious objection during the First World War includes the earliest, John W. Graham's *Conscription and Conscience* (Allen and Unwin, 1922, reprinted by Forgotten Books, 2012), and the new and ongoing work of Cyril Pearce, with its invaluable focus on, first, regional differences in attitudes to war and to conscientious objectors in *Comrades in Conscience* (Francis Boutle, 2001, new edition 2014) and second, on the recovery and listing of the names of COs throughout the country; his interactive database of already 20,000 will go online under the auspices of the Imperial War Museum in 2015.

Although it did not come out until 1980, I wrote *Bertrand Russell and the Pacifists* at an exciting time in the story of the Bertrand Russell Archives at McMaster University, and at a time when research followed a very different pattern from that of today. Completed in 1975, the original draft, written for my doctoral thesis, came together while the core material of the archives was still being sorted and while smaller additions – and often big surprises (what, yet another unknown lover?) – came in by every post.

I have recently read Nicholas Griffin's *A Pacifist at War* with enjoyment, not least because it took me back to the time when I went off to the University of Texas to read Bertie's letters to Ottoline Morrell, newly acquired, and not then available anywhere else. I spent a month at Austin, making notes (photocopying was not permitted), and thanking whatever powers there be that Russell had such legible handwriting. My focus was narrow; I wanted light on Russell's public pacifist activities. I can only rejoice that I did not have to take account of all the detail about his kaleidoscopic personal life revealed in Griffin's book. Yet although I barely skimmed his love letters, my narrative is indeed intensely personal. But the Conscientious Objectors are really the heroes of this story, and I think Russell would have wanted it to be so.

As it happened, the Russell Archives was only the takeoff point; most of my material was to be found elsewhere. Getting a grant to travel from the Canada Council, I went to the UK, dreaming vaguely of unearthing a complete archive of the No-Conscription Fellowship. I knew that the NCF kept duplicates of everything, for backup in case of government raids, and I thought that perhaps some major collection lurked forgotten in some obscure attic, somehow omitted from the wholesale voluntary purge that took place to preserve privacy and reputations at the end of the war. I never found it.

What I did find was something of at least equal value – as it turned out, I think, of greater value. I knew of Catherine Marshall as an important colleague of Russell's in the NCF, and I had already made my way to the Clifford Allen archive at the University of South Carolina, so when I learnt that her papers were in the Cumberland (now Cumbria) Record Office at Carlisle, I went there without delay.

The work Marshall had done with Russell probably played a large part in the preservation of her archive; at the time that a mass of more or less jumbled papers had been found in hampers in a shed at Hawse End, the family home of the Marshalls, near Keswick, in the English Lake District, she and her remarkable work for peace and for women had undeservedly faded from public memory. But manuscript recognisably in Russell's hand

and correspondence with many well known politicians were visible in the jumble, ensuring that the papers were rescued and taken into safe keeping in the Record Office. No funds were available for cataloguing them, so when I turned up, I was permitted to undertake the first sorting, with the blessing of the archivist, Bruce Jones. This unpaid task would occupy all my available time for a number of years, but by the end of that first summer (1969), I had most of the Russell material I needed, and returned to the Russell Archives with a vast load of photocopies and microfilm. The end notes of *Conscientious Objection* provide ample evidence of how important a source Marshall's papers were.

Later, I went back to complete the first sorting of the Marshall papers, and to begin research on other aspects of her life's work, the significance of which I had already begun to understand. My work and that of others who have used her papers has led to progress being made in reinstating her to the leading position which should be hers in both peace work and work for women's rights. This is not the place to tell in full how her story unfortunately exemplifies the dictum that history is told by the victors, but it is necessary and appropriate to comment on the part that Russell played in shrinking the picture of her work for the NCF, and distorting it.

Russell's first few months in the NCF had qualities which could not last, and could never be replicated. A particular kind of companionship comes when we work closely with a few others in a crisis situation, and Mephy (Russell's nickname), CA (Clifford Allen) and CEM (Catherine Marshall) had it in abundance for a few months in the early days of the implementation of the Military Service Act. Russell later forgot the intensity and the joy of the experience, but he left it on record in his letters to Ottoline Morrell.

In these early days, CA's role was to inspire, Russell's was to provide a name, to write letters and articles, to speak and to learn, CEM's was to organise, to provide knowledge of public personalities, to show how the system worked, and to be constantly on call. For Russell, she was in fact a mentor and a facilitator, enabling him to make use of his special gifts and providing the nitty-gritty of support. Russell appreciated her special skills and knowledge. These three called each other 'Comrade' and in their various roles rubbed along together informally and effectively, responding to crisis after crisis, until two things occurred to change the balance and the interaction. The first was CA's imprisonment, predictable and indeed delayed for longer than could have been expected. The second was the formalisation of their roles; the old Political Associates' Committee was gone and Russell and Marshall became part of the formal structure of the

NCF. At the end of 1916, both were candidates for the position of Acting Chair of the NCF; Russell took the position. She was still the one who best knew what needed to be done, but she tried to play the subordinate; he made a better administrator than he himself thought, but unconsciously retained some of the expectations normally attendant on his rank and position.

There is not much that I would change in how I depicted the relationship between Russell and Marshall. She did her best to support him in his work; he did a great deal initially to support her, both in her NCF work and in her private grief for Allen. Gradually, personal characteristics in each contributed to a deteriorating relationship. Under the pressure of too much work and diminished hope for a good outcome, her ever present compulsion to overwork escalated; but he never admitted that his complicated private life, his underlying yen to return to philosophy, and even an element of boredom with the tedious aspects of NCF work resulted in his failure at times to fulfil his obligations. Her 'cantankerous' letters were not wholly without justification. Russell's view of Catherine's work for the NCF was not shared by most of her colleagues, but there is no evidence that he ever regained his initial high opinion of her work; he never made an opportunity to pay tribute to what she had done for the Conscientious Objectors.

I find it inappropriate to end my introduction to the new edition on so negative a note. This is still the story of a great man, serving a vital cause in a remarkable way, by stepping completely outside any role that could have been forecast for him, a man who was born and bred to be an intellectual, an academic, an aristocrat, who was able to work alongside others in a very different world and for an unpopular cause.

*Jo Vellacott, **Conscientious Objection: Bertrand Russell and the Pacifists in the First World War**, Spokesman Books, new edition 2015, 340 pages, ISBN 9780851248424, £14.99*

'Jo Vellacott's excellent book is a model of careful scholarship, clear and lively writing, and the choice of a subject that matters deeply. One hundred years on, it's high time we honoured those who had the courage to speak out against the madness of the First World War and who suffered for doing so. It's a delight to see this volume available again.'

Adam Hochschild
author of the bestseller To End All Wars

Where Huddersfield Led

In January 1917, about twenty young men who attempted to disrupt a meeting in the Victoria Hall in Huddersfield were driven from the premises in ignominious defeat, among the cheers of the audience. Disruption of meetings was not uncommon at this time; in London, the *Daily Express* made a practice of announcing meetings of pacifist organisations in order to encourage rowdies to cause trouble. What is remarkable about this event is that the speaker was to be Philip Snowden, a notorious socialist pacifist Member of Parliament, and that it was the disrupters who lost out, not the pacifist supporters.

Cyril Pearce's remarkable book, *Comrades in Conscience,* provides an in-depth history of the background to the unusual public visibility of anti-war sentiment and, even more significantly, of tolerance for its expression that prevailed in Huddersfield. The book opens with a description of Huddersfield in 1914, but one that is in fact (and usefully) more of a history of how it came to be what it was, a graphic account of the rapid rise of a prosperous manufacturing town, and of its political development. Complexities abound, but, to simplify, what emerges is a picture of a city with a strongly Liberal political bent, although with a rising Conservative component, and a politically active working class, socialist in its sympathies, but itself uneasily divided in its allegiance to the Independent Labour Party (ILP), the British Socialist Party (BSP) and trade union loyalties.

Colouring Huddersfield's social history is a mix of nonconformist religion, paternalism, self-help, and co-operation. All of this made for a climate of vigorous, but on the whole respectful, controversy; everything was discussed publicly (and, by inference, privately) in meetings, adult schools, Socialist Sunday Schools, churches, the municipal council, trade unions, women's groups, fora of every political colour. The community was well served by its three newspapers, the *Examiner* (Liberal), the *Chronicle* (Conservative), and the *Worker* (Socialist). Again and again, as I read the description of Huddersfield before the war, I was struck by the vigour of the discussions that took place, on paper, in the press, at meetings, within organisations, in church groups, within trade unions, and at the municipal government level. All topics were up for discussion and opinion – social issues, political issues, ethical issues, and of course at the forefront, the issues of the day. The coming of war only intensified the vitality of these discussions and, if anything, widened the range of involvement.

In the summer of 1914 Huddersfield was experiencing a bitter strike in the engineering industry, the industrial field second only in that city to the multifaceted textile industry. Local interest was on this, and, in common with the rest of Britain, on the crisis in Ireland. As long as the cabinet in Westminster, unable to achieve unity, sat on its hands and made no public statement of its intentions, Huddersfield was part of the general picture of no more than detached interest in the antics of militarists in Europe. When it belatedly became clear that British intervention was a real possibility, Huddersfield was still not much different from the rest of Britain in the demonstrations that were held in favour of British neutrality.

When, suddenly, British involvement was a reality, the major Liberal press throughout the country made a complete turnaround, and began to talk in patriotic terms of the expectation that men would rush to the colours. A Liberal government had led Britain into the war, and so was now at pains to turn the war into a holy crusade; the Conservatives had long wanted this war; the Parliamentary Labour Party had fallen into line, only the Independent Labour Party stood out against the war. The Huddersfield *Examiner* competed with the *Chronicle* in its support for the war effort. But in this northern area the attempt did not resonate with all; internationalist thinking and a belief in progress towards a peaceful world had informed the thinking of many Liberals. Some middle-class Liberals found something in common with the socialist internationalism of many workers. Many socialists clung to their belief in international class solidarity as more relevant to them than any call to patriotism; the *Worker* continued to blame the militarist class for the war and to advocate for revolutionary change to put industry under the control of the workers.

Detailed local study provides a microscope under which to examine generalisations and myths about attitudes to the war. Pearce effectively demonstrates weaknesses in the myth that presents workers as having leapt to the support of the nation, giving up their previous investment in the class struggle. As he sees it, although socialist internationalism had not found the leaders who could draw it together across borders, nor had patriotism won out over the consciousness of the class struggle, which continued as an important factor in local industrial relations, not only in the known areas of unrest such as the Clyde, but throughout Yorkshire, and most visibly in Huddersfield. Rather than ready to make sacrifices in the name of patriotism, we see a work-force ready to exploit the government's urgent need for product, and the opportunities this provided for workers; several minor strikes in late 1914 and in 1915 won their objectives with comparative ease, and, of course, their employers were also benefiting from the boom in war production. Conscientious objectors (COs) were even sent to Huddersfield to perform such work; these were mainly those from religious organisations, such as the Christadelphians, whose emphasis was on the command not to kill but whose church approved their producing military clothing or even picric acid, used in detonators for bombs. Socialists, who were not willing to kill German conscripts, and Quakers, who opposed all use of violence, mostly rejected this form of alternative service.

During the early months of the war, while some bickering went on within, for instance, the Trades Council (a forum which brought together the various elements of labour opinion) actual opposition to the war effort was necessarily expressed more through inaction than through direct action, that is, by not volunteering for the armed forces. My previous study has been focused mainly on the national and London scene, where I have found opponents of the war struggling to find a place to express their views. Pearce shows something quite different in Huddersfield, presenting a vivid picture of open public discussion of the issues, with the pro-war elements having to create space for themselves in a climate where prevailing opinion was anti-war. A Huddersfield Workers' Own Recruiting Committee (HWORC) came into being, and provided a platform for some local leaders, but it seems to have been mainly the product of government action, and it remained largely ineffective, though rather more success was achieved on those occasions when recruiting was carried out with the help of a parade of soldiers, complete with regimental band. From the beginning of the war, the membership of the local Civilian Recruiting Committee had reinforced the sense of class division. Unable to draw in labour representatives (curiously, only one even from the HWORC), its efforts were mostly directed at employers and the Town Council, where they had some success in having men of military age laid off or pressured in other ways to volunteer for service. As elsewhere, departing recruits were seen off by crowds; even in these Pearce detects a more sober spirit than is depicted by mythology – and by some recent historians.

By the autumn of 1915, long casualty lists and the growing probability of conscription provided a focus for both pro and anti-war sentiment. In Huddersfield opposition was vocal, especially among workers and their organisations. Support for Liberalism in Huddersfield seems to have gone deeper than political support for the Liberal Party, entailing liberal values that made conscription hard to accept, even for some of those who reluctantly supported the war.

Something of the same dislike of compulsion had troubled the Cabinet;

indeed, the inclusion of the conscience clause in the Military Service Acts, when they were finally passed in 1916, was the child of liberal unease among those in power. The conscience clause was, in a very real sense, a breakthrough, but it was badly worded and obscure and led to a great deal of difficulty. Pearce's detailed examination of the functioning of the Huddersfield Tribunal is of considerable interest, enabling us to position it in the local political context, a rare opportunity. The exceptional tolerance to COs shown in Huddersfield seldom extended to the decisions of the tribunal, but did from time to time enable it unwillingly to serve as a forum for the expression of anti-war or anti compulsion opinion. In Huddersfield; COs might be publicly reviled by some, but so might those be who condemned them, and in general there was a warmth towards those who suffered for their opposition to the war, and for their families, similar to that felt for those who accepted conscription and went off to fight.

No one has looked more carefully or analytically at those who opposed conscription than Pearce, and it is interesting that in his examination of Huddersfield conscientious objectors, he did not find any congruence or overwhelming influence; they came with a wide variety of motivation, background, and political and religious orientation.

Was Huddersfield an anomaly, different from anywhere else? Or did what Pearce has uncovered as going on there occur in other places, which have however remained undocumented? The answer would seem to be both that Huddersfield was unique, and that there may well have been more resistance to the war throughout the country, and in particular in the north, than has previously been thought, and for which some of us have found scattered anecdotal evidence.

Pearce includes tables listing the diverse motivations and political and religious backgrounds of Huddersfield COs, a work that he has now extended to all COs in Britain, initiating the invaluable database, the *Pearce Register of British Conscientious Objectors*, which has been adopted by the Imperial War Museum as part of its *Lives of the First World War* collection. It may well be that this work will help answer some of the questions opened up by this important book.

Jo Vellacott

Cyril Pearce, Comrades In Conscience: The story of an English community's opposition to the Great War, *Francis Boutle Publishers, revised edition 2014, 304 pages, ISBN 9781903427828, £15 (www.francisboutle.co.uk)*

Ken Coates and socialist renewal

Tom Unterrainer

'It is all very well to agree that we are in favour of ... industrial democracy in Britain, a society planned and free, economically advanced but morally alive. It is even good to agree that we must not stand idly by ... The real question is, given all these things, what do we do next?*'*

A Future for British Socialism?
Ken Coates, 1968

In October 2012, I 'discovered' Ken Coates. I say 'discovered', but I'd heard of Ken more than ten years before this date in connection with anti-war campaigning. What I really mean is that I started to read and think about Ken's very many books, articles and his political activities.

The circumstances of this discovery are worth re-telling, if only because they demonstrate the reach and enduring influence of Ken's ideas. Leo Panitch – editor of the *Socialist Register*, student of Ralph Miliband, and eminent political economist –visited Nottingham to deliver a lecture on his book *The Making of Global Capitalism*. At the opening of the lecture, Panitch asked: 'who in the audience has heard of Ken Coates?' Despite knowing the name, I didn't raise my hand. Neither did anyone else in the room.

Panitch went on to explain that the last time he visited Nottingham was in the 1970s, whilst completing his PhD, and the sole purpose of the trip was to meet Ken. On this recommendation, I ordered a copy of Ken's collection of essays *Beyond Wage Slavery* and was captivated. Two things impressed me about the essays. Firstly, the constant challenges to the reader: 'what next?', 'if we can't do this what can we

The author is compiling an annotated bibliography of Ken Coates' extensive writings.

do?', 'why not?' These essays are no meander around some aspect of history or theory; they are sharply written expositions with a practical purpose in mind. Secondly, the range of ideas covered – democracy, education, the Labour Party, the Belgian General Strike, the environment – spoke of a socialist actively engaged in many causes. Particularly impressive is that, as early as 1972, Ken was writing about the environment in these terms:

> 'Industrial, political and social democracy are not … dispensable attitudes, transitory systems of administration. They must be at the very core of any strategy for the defence of [the] environment, if we are not to see a situation in which the very squalor of capitalism becomes a pretext for riveting its basic institutions and impulses even more firmly and inflexibly on an increasingly reluctant society.'
>
> *'Democracy and the Environment'*

Forty-three years later, we find Naomi Klein writing in similar terms in her book *This Changes Everything.*

First and foremost, through these essays Ken is addressing himself to the Labour Movement. The purpose of his writing is not to mobilise some lacuna of collective thought and compliance but to challenge and organise activity in the movement as a whole. As I was to discover, from the early 1960s onwards, Ken was involved in efforts to mobilise, organise and educate the Labour Movement on a socialist basis. There were several vehicles through which this was achieved: *The Week* – 'a news analysis for socialists', the Centre for Socialist Education, the *Voice* newspapers, a variety of conferences and meetings and, centrally, the Labour Party.Up until the later 1960s, Ken was a member of a variety of far-left groups and, together with Pat Jordan, founded what was to become the International Marxist Group. In the first years of the IMG's formation, *The Week* was the group's main publication, but its character was very different from what you might imagine the publication of a tiny radical group to be. First and foremost, it was in no way self-referential, self-aggrandising or other-worldly. *The Week* enjoyed sponsorship from a variety of Labour Movement figures, members of Parliament and socialist intellectuals. Under Ken's joint editorship of the journal with Robin Blackburn, the struggles of the global labour movement and oppressed peoples were projected into the consciousness of socialist activists in Britain. As Ken wrote in the Editorial of the first issue:

> 'Socialists today have a difficult and prodigious task in remaining both active as socialists and keeping conversant with the significance of a whole plethora of national and international events, large and small. In a world where a relatively

> minor occurrence in a small and little-known country like Laos has the potential of triggering events of nuclear and global significance, the need for detailed and accurate information in a precise and useful form cannot be denied.'

Throughout the 1960s, Ken and a growing band of comrades worked to make socialist ideas relevant to the realities of the British Labour Movement and to organise sharp interventions into the living and breathing organisations of this movement. Ken's attack on the Wilson government's supplicant relationship with the US over the war against Vietnam was not simply the outraged response of a morally offended individual, but the expression of a growing movement of discontent. The Institute for Workers' Control was not a political front marshalling imaginary battalions, but an organic expression of a substantial movement within the trade unions and Labour Movement more widely.

These activities were guided by a perspective rooted in the working class movement, informed by international events and concerns, inspired by contemporary intellectual developments, but driven by the imperative to make ideas a reality. This perspective endured and is neatly summarised in Ken's introduction to *How to Win? Labour versus unemployment*', published in 1981:

> 'The debate within the Labour Movement in the late nineteen seventies raised many crucial issues about political organisation. All of these are burningly relevant to the political economy of the late 'eighties. Their resolution is a task for a vast movement of people, not for a cabal of scholars. These people will be taking part in a transformation with implications for an area far wider than the geography of one small rainy island. All the signs are that the size of the challenge will condition the scope of the response.'

The full extent of Ken's influence and the individuals and organisations with whom he worked cannot be given justice in a few hundred words of reflection. Such a consideration is long overdue but the aim here is to start an urgent discussion. Ken Coates was not a guru, a prophet or messiah. His story does not provide all of the answers to all of the questions we now face. But Ken's work – his voluminous writings and political initiatives – is a vital reference point for those of us determined to build and renew the socialist movement in Britain. It is a vital reference point for those of us who see the connections between the continuing drive to war, environmental degradation, economic crisis, social cruelty and political dishonesty.

Ken's work is important because it demonstrates the historical existence of 'another socialism': a socialism rooted in practical reality, informed by international concerns and a sense of moral urgency. The work of renewing socialism can find no more powerful reference point than this.

Reviews

In place of fear?

John Hills, *Good Times, Bad Times: The welfare myth of them and us*, Policy Press, 2015, 334 pages, paperback ISBN 9781447320036, £10.39
Mary O'Hara, *Austerity Bites: A journey to the sharp end of cuts in the UK*, Policy Press, 2014, 320 pages, hardback ISBN 9781447315605, £15.99

One million people in Britain, one of the wealthiest countries in the western world, regularly rely on charity donations to put food on the table. Millions more struggle to heat their homes. Deciding whether to eat or heat defines their daily existence. What is the government's response? It accuses them of wanting something for nothing, 'food for free' and has redefined 'fuel poverty' so that far fewer appear to be left in the cold. Two powerful but very different books are essential to understanding how this has happened, with the Conservative and Liberal Democrat Coalition Government deliberately dismantling the welfare state over the last five years as part of its planned 'austerity' measures.

Many of the cuts the Coalition has made have been justified on targeted cost grounds: in the case of the welfare state '…the poor got too expensive'. At the same time, it has convinced the public that 'we' (the tax-paying 'strivers') are shelling out in taxes to maintain a feckless, unchanging dependent underclass. Seen from this perspective, redistribution, a central feature of the welfare state, is an unjustifiable handout: cutting back on 'welfare' is both essential and 'fair' to everyone. Award-winning *Guardian* journalist Mary O'Hara's shocking account of the personal impact of these attacks on the poorest, shows the devastating human cost of a range of vicious Coalition austerity measures while John Hills' meticulous, highly accessible analysis of the British welfare state goes much further – demolishing Coalition myths designed to divide and antagonise 'us' from the deliberately stigmatised 'them'. He demonstrates that the Coalition's approach has been costly, regressive and profoundly inept.

The poorest have been hit the hardest by cuts in welfare benefits and local government services but there are wider ramifications for all of us. The future of the welfare state as we know it is now seriously under threat from a government that wants permanent austerity and the minimal state.

Mary O'Hara was grant-aided in 2012 by the Joseph Rowntree Foundation (JRF) and the charity Locality, to travel the country interviewing those most directly affected by cuts in benefits and services. She produced 18 audio-visual reports on this work which are available on the JRF website. Her book *Austerity bites* was written to provide a wider context to those reports and to give voice to people who wanted to be heard but who believe they are being deliberately ignored by the politicians who are wreaking havoc on their lives and their communities. As 'Annie' from Birmingham said:

'I can't think straight when the government cuts certain things. I don't know how they come to these decisions. I don't think they live in the real world. They're cutting benefits people need to survive.'

Hundreds of hours of interviews have been condensed into chapters which focus on the rise of food poverty and food 'banks'; the growth of financial insecurity for people in low-paid jobs, often with zero-hours contracts or sham self-employment; the advent of 'Wongaland' and escalation of borrowing from illegal loan-sharks; the devastating effects of welfare benefit 'sanctions' on people left with no money for weeks at a time; the communities where social housing now stands empty because families have been forced out because of the bedroom tax with no-one suitable on the waiting list to move in; and the appalling treatment of sick and disabled people under the government's flagship 'Work Programme'. One example:

Work Capability assessor: 'Are you suicidal'

Benefits claimant: 'Yes'

Assessor: 'Well then, why haven't you achieved it?'

There is much more. O'Hara not only reports from across the UK. She also has tapped into a wide range of academic and policy reports to provide a broad picture. The book was prepared in late 2013 so has to be updated by the reader in some instances but that by no means detracts from each chapter. For example, more recent substantial criticisms of the Work Programme now abound in the press and Parliament.

John Hills is a Professor of Social Policy at the London School of Economics. The work on which his book, *Good Times, Bad Times,* is based has been funded by a prestigious research institute and is focused on the design of policy relating to the welfare state. Consequently, Hills retains most of his direct political criticism to the last chapter but, inevitably, he has to start his account of the role of the welfare state by first discussing the way in which Coalition politicians have created the divisive language of 'us' and 'them' ('strivers' and 'skivers'/ 'Benefits Street' versus 'alarm-clock Britain') which they use to justify significant policy changes and substantial reductions to welfare benefit entitlements or 'welfare', as they choose to describe our welfare state. This is an Americanism that is an indicator of how Coalition politicians would like the British welfare state to substantially reduce to a stigmatised version of the US system.

Two fictional families are used by Hills throughout the book to show how the welfare state works in more detail. Wealthy Henrietta and Stephen Osborne live in an owner-occupied home in prosperous Alderley Edge in Cheshire. Struggling Jim and Tracey Ackroyd live in their council home in Salford, Greater Manchester. Their extended families, including children and grandchildren, were first created for ITV's World in Action 'Spongers' (1989) and took the form of a spoof game-show designed to reveal the real welfare state 'spongers'. Surprisingly, in 1989, over their whole lives, the 'university educated, opera-loving middle-class' Osborne family proved to be the winners. But who would win now after five years of austerity?

Accounts of each families' fortunes over time are used as an introduction to each chapter: specific generations of each family vividly demonstrating their financial gains and losses, from their earned income and tax liabilities, any welfare benefit entitlements, the use of other welfare state services, like NHS hospitals (which are costed for this exercise), and their savings and wealth accumulation more generally. These are discussed in much more detail in each chapter, making extensive use of survey data from a wide range of sources (including large government surveys) to show whether these fictional circumstances are typical or atypical. This broad way of analysing what the welfare state does for particular families at different ends of the income distribution are designed to capture the idea that the safety net or redistributive role of the welfare state, including welfare benefits and state pensions, NHS health and state education, operate over different time scales and in varying circumstances. These distinct chapters are followed by a more wide-ranging discussion about the ever-changing backdrop of the economy (specifically the effect of inflation, economic growth and recession) and societal change (especially increases in the numbers of older people).

Despite all the political rhetoric claiming that the poor are too expensive, the wealthy Osbornes receive by far the most financial help from the welfare state (and the state generally through favourable tax treatments) across their lifetimes compared to the Ackroyds, whose low income skirts the poverty line for most of their lives. Hills takes the long view in considering these families, and for the Osbornes includes favourable tax treatment of property ownership (the now-abolished mortgage interest tax relief), pension saving and other investments, as well as the money they save on otherwise expensive private education and hospital treatment. This moves us away from simple snapshots of benefit entitlements which have been deliberately distorted by the Coalition (often including housing benefit which is used to pay the landlord's rent) to make them look more generous than they are and to justify cutbacks or caps.

When considering the complex ways in which the welfare state interacts with different families at different times, Hills demonstrates that the redistributive element of the welfare state partly flows within families (families benefit roughly in line with their tax contributions over their lifetimes) as well as between generations (younger working age households contribute to the welfare benefits and services used by the older generation such as social care, but will themselves benefit in turn likewise). And, of course, redistribution also takes place in a more straightforward sense, too, from richer households to the poorest through progressive taxation.

Why do those on average and middle incomes feel they have lost out? John Hills shows that, despite the welfare state, Britain remains one of the six most unequal countries in the industrialised world (only Chile and Ireland are worse in relation to income inequality). The different arms of the welfare state (health, education, social care, housing, pensions, welfare benefits) all struggle to make an impact in reducing inequalities because there is so much to do compared to other countries. The situation has worsened recently but that is not because the poor have become too expensive. The proportionate value of welfare benefits and public services to the poorest fifth of the population (about 13 million people) has stayed much the same since 1979. In fact, since then, the overall income distribution has been decreasing for four-fifths of the population (which includes the poorest up to those with middle incomes). It will now be no surprise to learn that the share in income of the top fifth of the population has increased (from 35% in 1979 to 42% in 2010-11) and most of that increase has gone to the super-rich 1%. The reality is that middle incomes have not been squeezed by the poorest but by the richest. The richest continue to gain enormously from investment income and favourable tax arrangements, have not contributed through tax on a par with everyone else, and have not been affected by austerity measures. If anyone has become too expensive for the country, Hills argues, it is the very rich.

Both authors also discuss what Mary O'Hara describes as the Coalition's 'relentless vilification' of the poor and vulnerable, which has affected public opinion. She writes a blistering analysis of the impact of this and has a specific chapter on how it has affected sick and disabled people. She makes the point strongly that the government's barrage of negative description and deliberate distortion has been taken up by most of the mainstream media. She refers to a *Guardian* newspaper analysis in April 2013 of the previous year's government communications, which found increasing use of pejorative and value-laden language when referring to benefits and welfare. The media were equally culpable. During the same time, the term 'benefit cheat' was used 442 times in national newspapers, an increase of almost two-thirds compared to the 12 months up to the change of government in 2010.

Given this, it is hardly surprising that the attitude of many of those working in stable employment or on good retirement income has hardened, while many of the poorest have despaired. Most of the public have no idea how the welfare state works, who it is helping and, most importantly, the extent of fraud in the system. For example, it is now widely believed by the public that far more is paid in Job-Seekers Allowance (JSA) for the unemployed than state retirement pensions. JSA actually makes up 3% of total welfare benefits expenditure while expenditure on state pensions is 15 times more (£4.9 billion compared to £74.2 billion). People surveyed by IPSOS Mori in 2012 had no realistic idea of the extent of fraud either: the average amount that people thought was fraudulently claimed from all benefits and tax credits was £27 in every £100. The Department of Work and Pensions' official figure for fraud is 70p in every £100 (£1.7 billion for the whole benefit system including pensions while £1.6 billion was underpaid as a result of official error). As Hills points out, this puts us behind only Turkey, Italy, Greece and Poland in our belief that our compatriots are on the fiddle.

Why does this matter? It matters because the Coalition has created and used a simple narrative that has been taken on board by the media and many of the British public. It suggests that the welfare state is overblown and too expensive, riddled with 'dependency', and used simply by people who want 'something for nothing'. This prepares the ground for even more swingeing cutbacks, all in the direction of the completely inadequate US system. All of us will lose out, including pensioners, if that happens. John Hills' book provides an accurate and long-overdue detailed analysis of the welfare state, but it may only be read by policy specialists and people in academia. Mary O'Hara's book provides the emotional counterblast to Coalition myths, foregrounding real people whom these cuts are affecting now. It makes for powerful and profoundly upsetting reading, but will politicians and their advisors read it? Many she spoke to believe that politicians are out of touch and are not interested in the damage that is being done to individuals, families and communities up and down the land. As one person commented:

'When Aneurin Bevan and his people were setting about the task of ensuring that we could all live in a safe community their phrase was "in place of fear". What we have returning now is fear – fear of the unknown, fear of destitution and fear of poverty.'

But she also found that many believed that there was a limit to cutbacks that could be made. People could only bear so much and many were angry even as they struggled on. Her last chapter discusses some of the campaigning that had taken place up to 2013 and which continues: national, regional, city wide, specialist and profoundly local opposition to cuts and sanctions. The last word in the book goes to Sharon from Croxteth:

'There's the prime example of the ants and the polar bear. The ant comes over and says "Excuse me, can you move?" And the polar bear just [ignores him]. So he goes away and comes back with 3,000 of his friends and he says "Excuse me!" and the polar bear gets up and moves. And I think that's what it is with people. People feel they are on their own and they're not going to get listened to. They need to get together to make people listen to them.'

Cathy Davis

Killer Asbestos

Jan Cremers, Rolf Gehring (editors), *The long and winding road to an asbestos free workplace*, International Books, European Institute for Construction Labour Research (CLR Studies 7), 2013, 160 pages, paperback ISBN 9789057271069, £24

The title of this book pays a little homage to pop culture of the 1960s and that, you would expect, is as close as this subject can get to celebrity culture. Then, in a section entitled 'a workers' disease' it finishes with

> 'The media coverage of asbestos is equally illuminating: the death of Steve McQueen ['Bullitt', 'The Thomas Crown Affair' and other films: reviewer's inclusion, for information only], who was exposed to asbestos in his youth working on dismantling ships, attracts more headlines than the millions of workers killed over nearly 150 years.'

This highlights in a single snapshot the ongoing tragedy and indiscriminate nature of deaths from exposure to asbestos regardless of who you are. This is only the second book I have read cover-to-cover on this subject. The first was *Asbestos, Killer Dust* (BSSRS Publications), which set out the case against asbestos and how best to fight this hazard. It examined the record of government, industry, unions, scientists and doctors in this regard. Most of its case studies and information were gleaned from UK experience.

The long and winding road to an asbestos free workplace can clearly be stated to agree with the assertions of the earlier title, and develops its own arguments and insights into not only the asbestos industry of the UK, but also from a truly global perspective. There is a huge amount of work underpinning this slight volume and an equally huge story to be told. The attitude of the asbestos industry is no surprise and is forensically laid out here, where their goal is money, money, and more money, and hang the cost. Sadly, they are not the only parties subject to a deeply critical analysis, as trades unions, workers and governments worldwide are exposed as having been indifferent, slow and, in some surprising instances, obstructive to the implementation of at least some safety measures.

It is usually the case for trades unions to campaign to protect jobs, and for workers to be concerned if their role is threatened. But I was shocked at the lack of insight into the bigger picture of worker health, with some almost not wishing to know the harsh reality of working with asbestos. However, when people are elected to political positions and become part of government they are supposedly charged with a duty of care for the population of their country, not just economically, but also with business and worker health. It is therefore deeply disturbing to see governments actively pursuing the reckless reintroduction of asbestos by attempting to exploit new and emerging markets, where there is not the regulation to offer protections to the workers, who will therefore become the next generation of cancer sufferers as a direct consequence of exposure to asbestos. This book underlines and reinforces all the great and hard work done by campaigners against asbestos from the newly awakened trades unions, government departments, and some workers.

The one abiding point is that this campaign has been both local and global at the same time. *The long and winding road to an asbestos free workplace* clearly outlines that the campaign has not been a single march to a bright new future; more an ebb and flow of success and failure as the asbestos industry has put in place organisations and individuals to obfuscate the arguments, obliterate ideas and, when that fails, simply to stall and delay by legal process any action that could stem its business 'success'.

This book explains in a simple, clear, unemotional way how, when governments, trades unions and workers campaign and fight, both locally and globally, they can successfully take on the clearly failing neoliberal capitalist agenda. Should anyone now believe that ANY business in ANY market should be left to regulate itself, then look at this book and the examples it exposes of the conduct of national and international business. Fundamentally, neo-liberalism is about filleting all and any governmental administration, legislation or regulation that limits, controls or stops any business from maximising its profits. Neoliberals neither care about nor are concerned for their workers' welfare. They have no concern for the damage they do to the planet, and have no interest in mitigating their actions, as that would impact on their profits. *The long and winding road to an asbestos free workplace* elegantly lays that bare in the asbestos industry. Where the actions of the asbestos industry are shown here to circumvent, stop and damage any opposition to their objectives, you can see a model of behaviour and a formula that has either been used or garnered from other industries to apply across all industries.

The attacks on workers' health in the asbestos industry result in killer cancers such as mesothelioma. We are yet to see all the damage other workers may suffer from different businesses using the neoliberal model. Governments and some trades unionists may be as laid back in their initial approaches as they were in the asbestos case, as shown here. None the less, once their campaigns begin, there are millions of conscientious, hard-working people who will vigorously oppose their colleagues and their own damage at the hands of these criminal industrialists.

Robert Baer's book *See No Evil,* about his time in the CIA, was turned into the superb film 'Syriana'. Could we find another Grant Heslov and George Clooney to do the same with this book? It has the same up-close and personal stories such as Wilf Penney, head of The Asbestos Information Centre, a propaganda unit for asbestos manufacturers and producers, who after decades of denouncing arguments opposed to the use of asbestos felt he had to declare to Stephen Hughes MEP, on the opposite side of the argument, that he was right, as Penney was dying of mesothelioma. This was a very sad and personal irony, indeed.

The long and winding road to an asbestos free workplace is, first and foremost, a book about the asbestos industry and the global campaigning and opposition to the use of asbestos. It is also, in its own small way, an exposé of the conduct of the neoliberal business model with its one and only concern, profit at any cost.

Dave Putson

Fear and Loathing

James Delingpole, *Watermelons: How Environmentalists are Killing the Planet, Destroying the Economy and Stealing Your Children's Future*, Biteback Publishing, 2012, 320 pages, ISBN 9781849544054, £9.99

James Delingpole writes a regular column for *The Spectator*. His polemic, *Watermelons*, is an interesting if unpleasant book. He hates the green-ecology-environmental movements. He loathes the World Wide Fund for Nature (WWF), Greenpeace, Friends of the Earth. He scoffs at the idea of earth warming and climate change because of our super-production of carbon. Understandably, he objects to being called a climate change denier because of the overtones of 'Holocaust denier'.

Just follow the evidence, he says, rather than the money and pseudo-science. 'Green', he argues, is a huge industry, corrupted by huge vested interests. Those not on his side, he contemptuously calls 'greenies'. Yet, he provides a lot of evidence, obviously the result of a good deal of research, which I would like to see honestly, properly and scientifically refuted before I reject his point of view. That means proper evidence as against smears, though he is no mean smearer himself.

Delingpole denounces Rachel Carson's *The Silent Spring* and the campaign against and the prohibition of DDT insecticide. All nonsense, he says.

> 'Yet Gore and his ilk seem blissfully ignorant of the Environmental Protection Agency's seven-month hearing (and more than nine thousand pages of testimony) prior to the ban being enacted in which EPA Judge Edmund Sweeney concluded:
>
> "DDT is not a carcinogenic harmful to humans… DDT is not a mutagenic or teratogenic hazard to man… The use of DDT under the regulations involved here does not have a deleterious effect on freshwater fish, estuarine organisms, wild birds or other wildlife."'

Well, blow me over with a hammer. I had always believed that DDT weakened egg shells so birds couldn't breed successfully, and entered mother's breast milk and wasn't good for baby. He claims the prohibition of DDT is a kind of genocide because it has caused the deaths of millions from malaria and dengue fever, which could have been prevented.

Still, it is always good to have one's cherished beliefs and opinions challenged. I read *The Spokesman* to confirm them, not unsettle them; it broadens and deepens my life view. Yet, I go along with James because so many of my own sacred cows, through personal experience and research, have been found to have feet, legs and thighs of clay.

Delingpole has a message worth listening to, but he also has his own agenda. He wants to go on living the good life. He dismisses oil spills. A few thousand oil-soaked birds die – so what? He mentions, in passing, the loss of livelihoods for fishermen and seafood restaurateurs, but it's no big deal. Like all middle-class intellectuals, he knows all about poverty, but nothing of it.

Of course, there is climate change. The climate has always been changeable. He points to the medieval time of global warming (there were no smoking factories) and, nearer to our own times, 'The Great Cold', when the Thames froze over and fairs were held on ice. I can also remember smog so thick that I had to grope my way along a road and often found myself feeling my way up a strange garden drive. It was really that bad. It seems that the clean air acts did a good job clearing up this environmental mess, and deaths from respiratory distress among the very old and young declined. Remember, there were several million coal fires burning.

Mr. Delingpole denies that the clean air acts made much difference: the smog wipe-outs were on the decline anyway. This is an argument that interests me because it is one I have often used myself against vaccinations, e.g. polio was long in decline before Salk came along and the vaccine actually exacerbated the problem as polio re-adjusted itself to attack on another front. So, maybe, I should think again.

But then the author spoils his case by starting to get nasty. In the first half of the book he marshals a lot of evidence against global warming. However, like most technical evidence, it tends to be dry, boring and heavy going. So he tries to lighten it up by playing 'the cheeky chappie'. It doesn't work – he can no more bring it off than I am Max Miller. Obviously, he is afraid of being a boring, plodding intellectual who may have something important and interesting to say, so he goes into attack mode in the second half of the book and, I would say, spoils his own argument.

He is strongly anti-left; hence his unpleasant title, *Watermelons* (green on the outside, red on the inside) – apparently, all lefties are 'greenies' and all 'greenies' are 'lefties'. Is that true? Ask Prince Charles, whom he mocks mercilessly for his organic farming.

And this is when the author's smears really get going: the Nazis were 'greenies' too, not just the lefties. Hitler liked his soggy bowl of muesli for breakfast instead of a manly plate of bacon and eggs. Himmler was a vegetarian (so, are all vegetarians Nazis?) What on earth does this have to do with his argument? It's like saying Stalin smoked a pipe so all pipe-smokers are Stalinists.

Delinpole should get his own house in order: admit that he likes his own, comfy, professional, middle-class lifestyle (as we all do) and is not too bothered about the suffering masses who make it possible. It suits him, see. He should stick to the scientific facts he is keen on and not muddy them with his own prejudices, fears and loathing.

Nigel Potter
Honduras

Malaya Emergency

Christopher Hale, *Massacre in Malaya: Exposing Britain's My Lai,* The History Press, 2013, 432 pages, hardback ISBN 978 0 75248701 4, £25.00

This book is an exhaustive study of the British involvement in Malaya up until the inception of Malaysia, and is a useful addition to our knowledge of the reality that was the British Empire. It also questions aspects of the dominant narrative that the British military had some special expertise in counter-insurgence as exemplified by their conduct in the Malayan Emergency context. It goes without saying that this was a brutal war, like other liberation struggles which linked political with economic independence. The reviewer recalls a remark by Ken Coates that his decision to work as a face-worker in the Nottinghamshire coalfield was guided, in part, by his desire 'not to be sent to kill Malayan communists'.

Surprisingly, given the title of the book, the massacre at Batang Kali forms only one chapter, with most of the text devoted to a fascinating and extensive political history of Malaya, concentrating on the period from the Japanese invasion to the end of the Emergency. Britain had important economic interests in Malaya and, after dislodging other European rivals, was initially content to leave the administrative over-sight to the East India Company. As long as its trading and extractive activities were undisturbed, then the Sultans (titular heads of the internal Malayan states) who formed 'a compliant "native" elite', together with a British advisory 'resident', could see to the exploitation of this great colonial asset.

These assets were gold, tin, tapioca, gambier, pepper, coffee and, later, perhaps the most lucrative of all, rubber. Chinese migrants fleeing from the turmoil in southern China worked in the tin and gold mines, and working in the plantations were Tamils and poorer Malays. In general the life of these workers was one of gross exploitation: forced, indentured labour was common. Malayan society was therefore ethnically divided and this was reinforced by the racial division of labour.

By 1895, Malaya had become a federated Crown Colony with a Federal Council: its earlier relationship with the East India Company ended in 1858 with the Indian Mutiny. The corollary of this was the development of oppositional nationalist elements, sadly often on an ethnic basis. The Chinese formed the backbone of the Malayan Communist Party (MCP), which was not formally established until its first congress in 1930, facilitated by a certain Comintern agent, one Ho Chi Minh. However, the party had the unfortunate handicap of electing as general secretary, Lai Tek, a triple spy. 'Turned' by the French, he informed for both the British special branch and later for the Japanese, and then for the British again. Although idealised by party members, he connived in the murder of many of them. In fact, *Massacre in Malaya* has quite a lot to say about the role of Lai Tek, Mr. Wright to the British.

The limits of British power were graphically exposed by the fall of Singapore to the Japanese, in 1942, and whilst, initially, the conquerors were prepared to indulge the 'native' Malays, this was not the case with the persecuted Chinese. The Chinese formed the majority of the Malayan Peoples' Anti-Japanese Army (MPAJA), which was MCP instigated (later, many of its cadres were to form the Malayan National Liberation Army or MNLA). The returning British found a situation fraught with race riots against the Chinese by 'native' Malays and strikes, on which, strangely, Hale comments little. The British War Cabinet agreed to 'reform' the pre-war constitutional Federation, fearing that radical elements would capitalise on the disenfranchisement, the poverty, and lack of political power of the Chinese, Tamil and aboriginal minorities. They attempted to nullify the power of the Sultans and 'native' Malays and place *all* citizens on an equal footing. The opposition to such proposals was vociferous and included the old colonial British mine and plantation managers and owners. So strong was the opposition that the new Union had to be abandoned, with a reversion to the old statutes, which conferred alien status on the Chinese and Tamil citizens. Of course, imperialist powers have a partiality for utilising ethnic divisions ('divide and rule'), and this was a factor in Malaya's history, but it was to became a handicap when the need for a pliant, post-colonial independent nation was required.

On their return to Malaya, the British were keen to nip any communist insurrection in the bud and made preparations to suppress the Malayan Communist Party – the Emergency was no knee-jerk reaction. Could the nationalists have seized power before the British came back, as happened in neighbouring Burma? The new party leader, Chin Peng, was probably not disposed to such a policy, given the disunity of the various shades of nationalism. After three years of Japanese occupation, food was in short supply, unemployment was widespread, wages low, and inter-ethnic tension ran high. The MCP was not fully prepared for insurrection, which was pre-empted by the killing of three British plantation managers. This was the stated reason for the imposition of the 'Federal Emergency Regulations Ordinance' banning the MCP, in 1947.

The Emergency was to last, off and on, until 1989, but the major phase ended about four years after an unsuccessful attempt at a settlement in 1956. Initially, following the Maoist dictum, the MNLA established two 'liberated' safe areas, but they were unable to sustain them for any length of time. MNLA tactics therefore relapsed into hit and run attacks, emerging from the jungle to kill informers, and attack troops and police from ambush positions when possible. The British were to mount search and destroy forays into the jungle, but they were often unsuccessful and meant they became involved in actions against civilians such as the massacre of 24 plantation workers at Batang Kali. This massacre, on 19 March 1948, took place when a platoon of British soldiers entered the Chinese 'squatters' camp and, having systematically divided the women and children from the men, the latter were executed for no identifiable reason. The relatives of the murdered men instigated investigations and legal actions in Malaysia and the United Kingdom.

In 2009, the British Government rejected a call for a public enquiry. Subsequently, the High Court ruled that, although culpability lay with the UK, owing to a conflict in law between the House of Lords case law and the European Court of Human Rights, it could not agree to a public inquiry as the families of the victims desired.

The question as to who ordered the massacre is still unclear, but the two sergeants leading the platoon were interviewed by *The People* newspaper, and, in 1992, the BBC broadcast a documentary on the massacre called *In Cold Blood*. Perhaps a quotation from Sir Gerald Templar, 'The Tiger of Malaya', High Commissioner for part of the period of the Emergency, sets the matter in the context of the times:

> 'the hard core of armed communists in this country are fanatics and must be, and will be, exterminated.'

Templar was the replacement High Commissioner for his assassinated predecessor, Sir Henry Gurney.

The conflict between the Chinese and the 'native' Malays weakened support for the MNLA: they had to rely on support largely from the so-called Chinese 'squatters'. As a result, the 'squatters' were resettled away from the areas of MNLA activity and placed in 'resettlement camps', which had barbed wire perimeters and armed guards. Isolated from support, the MNLA troops slowly began to starve. This had a drastic effect on morale, and was a factor leading to disputes on tactics and also to criticism of the party leadership and their perks. Criticism of the leadership was not silenced with the 'semi-judicial murder of one of the party's most admired and eloquent theoreticians'. New tactics were formulated in the so-called 'October Directives', when the party was instructed to abandon 'violent tactics which have antagonised peasants and workers'. The disaffection in the MNLA ranks cannot have been helped by the problems of communication and isolation between the party and MNLA fighters. The heavy fatalities must all have affected morale – in 1951, MNLA troops numbered 8,000: this fell to 2,000 by 1957. Of course, the latter were drastically outnumbered by Commonwealth troops and local police.

The Malayan Emergency is often quoted as the textbook example of how to defeat an insurgency and, certainly, the Americans in Vietnam took it as a model. But, as *Massacre in Malaya* makes clear, this is not as straightforward as it appears – there existed a number of special factors that applied to the Malaya Emergency only. Of course, the Americans copied the resettlement idea in the form of the infamous 'strategic hamlets' policy in Vietnam, and the Emergency saw the first use of the toxic 'Agent Orange' defoliant. Unlike Malaya, the Vietnamese had the benefit of a relatively homogenous population and safe zones in Cambodia and the border with North Vietnam, whereas the MNLA was surrounded by hostile powers or physical barriers.

Massacre in Malaya is a veritable mountain of information, but I am afraid the sequencing of events leaves something to be desired, and a tendency to digress does confuse. The author is to be congratulated for the mighty labour of research he must have done, but I would suggest a non-specialist reader must have a sound grasp of the territory under discussion before launching themselves into the text. Finally, it would have been most helpful to be able to refer to a chronology of the major events and to a list of acronyms. A selection of maps to enlighten the reader is available at http://malayan.blogspot.de.

John Daniels

The European Theatre

Richard Sakwa, *Frontline Ukraine: Crisis in the Borderlands*, I. B. Tauris, 2014, 320 pages, hardback ISBN 9781784530648, £18.99

When Arseniy Yatsenyuk, Ukraine's prime minister, told a German TV station recently that the Soviet Union invaded Germany, was this just blind ignorance? Or a kind of perverted wishful thinking? If the USSR really was the aggressor in 1941, it would suit Yatsenyuk's narrative of current geopolitics in which Russia is once again the only side that merits blame.

When Grzegorz Schetyna, Poland's deputy foreign minister, said Ukrainians liberated Auschwitz, did he not know that the Red Army was a multinational force in which Ukrainians certainly played a role but the bulk of the troops were Russian? Or was he looking for a new way to provoke the Kremlin?

Faced with these irresponsible distortions, and they are replicated in a hundred other prejudiced comments about Russian behaviour from western politicians as well as their eastern European colleagues, it is a relief to find a book on the Ukrainian conflict that is cool, balanced and well sourced. Richard Sakwa makes repeated criticisms of Russian tactics and strategy, but he avoids lazy Putin-bashing and locates the origins of the Ukrainian conflict in a quarter-century of mistakes since the Cold War ended. In his view, three long-simmering crises have boiled over to produce the violence that is engulfing eastern Ukraine. The first is the tension between two different models of Ukrainian statehood. One is what he calls the 'monist' view, which asserts that the country is an autochthonous cultural and political unity and that the challenge of independence since 1991 has been to strengthen the Ukrainian language, repudiate the tsarist and Soviet imperial legacies, reduce the political weight of Russian-speakers, and move the country away from Russia towards 'Europe'. The alternative 'pluralist' view emphasises the different historical and cultural experiences of Ukraine's various regions and argues that building a modern democratic post-Soviet Ukrainian state is not just a matter of good governance and rule of law at the centre. It also requires an acceptance of bilingualism, mutual tolerance of different traditions, and devolution of power to the regions.

More than any other change of government in Kiev since 1991, the overthrow of Viktor Yanukovych last year brought the triumph of the monist view, held most strongly in western Ukraine, whose leaders were determined this time to ensure the winner takes all.

The second crisis arises from the internationalisation of the struggle inside

Ukraine, which turned it into a geopolitical tug of war. Sakwa argues that this stems from the asymmetrical end of the Cold War, which shut Russia out of the European alliance system. While Mikhail Gorbachev and millions of other Russians saw the end of the Cold War as a shared victory which might lead to the building of a 'common European home', most western leaders saw Russia as a defeated nation whose interests could be brushed aside, and which must accept US hegemony in the new single-superpower world order or face isolation. Instead of dismantling NATO, the Cold War alliance was strengthened and expanded in spite of repeated warnings from western experts on Russia that this would create new tensions. Long before Putin came to power, Yeltsin had urged the West not to move NATO eastwards.

Even today at this late stage, a declaration of Ukrainian non-alignment as part of an internationally negotiated settlement, and UN Security Council guarantees of that status, would bring instant de-escalation and make a lasting ceasefire possible in eastern Ukraine.

The hawks in the Clinton administration ignored all this, Bush abandoned the anti-ballistic missile treaty and put rockets close to Russia's borders, and now a decade later, after Russia's angry reaction to provocations in Georgia in 2008 and Ukraine today, we have what Sakwa rightly calls a 'fateful geographical paradox: that NATO exists to manage the risks created by its existence'.

The third crisis, also linked to the NATO issue, is the European Union's failure to stay true to the conflict resolution imperative that had been its original impetus. After 1989 there was much talk of the arrival of the 'hour of Europe'. Just as the need for Franco-German reconciliation inspired the EU's foundation, many hoped the Cold War's end would lead to a broader east-west reconciliation across the old Iron Curtain. But the prospect of greater European independence worried key decision-makers in Washington, and NATO's role has been, in part, to maintain US primacy over Europe's foreign policy. From Bosnia in 1992 to Ukraine today, the last two decades have seen repeated occasions where US officials pleaded, half-sincerely, for a greater European role in handling geopolitical crises in Europe while simultaneously denigrating and sidelining Europe's efforts. Last year's 'Fuck the EU' comment by Victoria Nuland, Obama's neocon assistant secretary of state for European and Eurasian affairs, was the pithiest expression of this.

Sakwa writes with barely suppressed anger of Europe's failure, arguing that instead of a vision embracing the whole continent, the EU has become little more than the civilian wing of the Atlantic alliance.

Within the framework of these three crises, Sakwa gives the best analysis yet in book form of events on the ground in eastern Ukraine as well as in Kiev, Washington, Brussels and Moscow. He covers the disputes between the 'resolvers' (who want a negotiated solution) and the 'war party' in each capital. He describes the rows over sanctions that have split European leaders, and points out how Ukraine's president, Petro Poroshenko, is under constant pressure from Nuland's favourite Ukrainian, the more militant Yatsenyuk, to rely on military force.

As for Putin, Sakwa sees him not so much as the driver of the crises but as a regulator of factional interests and a temporiser who has to balance pressure from more right-wing Russian nationalists as well as from the insurgents in Ukraine, who get weapons and help from Russia but are not the Kremlin's puppets.

Frontline Ukraine highlights several points that have become almost taboo in western accounts: the civilian casualties in eastern Ukraine caused by Ukrainian army shelling; the physical assaults on leftwing candidates in last year's election; and the failure to complete investigations of last February's sniper activity in Kiev (much of it thought to have been by anti-Yanukovych fighters) or of the Odessa massacre, in which dozens of anti-Kiev protesters were burnt alive in a building set on fire by nationalists.

The most disturbing novelty of the Ukrainian crisis is the way Putin and other Russian leaders are routinely demonised. At the height of the Cold War, when the dispute between Moscow and the West was far more dangerous, backed as it was by the danger of nuclear catastrophe, Brezhnev and Andropov were never treated to such public insults by western commentators and politicians.

Equally alarming, though not new, is the one-sided nature of western political, media and think-tank coverage. The spectre of senator Joseph McCarthy stalks the stage, marginalising those who offer a balanced analysis of why we have got to where we are and what compromise could save us. I hope Sakwa's book does not itself become a victim, condemned as insufficiently anti-Russian to be reviewed.

Jonathan Steele

With grateful acknowledgements to The Guardian

Here Comes the Bribe!

Nicholas Gilby, *Deception in High Places: A History of Bribery in Britain's Arms Trade*, Pluto Press, 2014, 240 pages, ISBN 9780745334264, £14

For a book on a decade-spanning, convoluted subject, *Deception in High*

Places puts its point across quite directly. Nicholas Gilby opens with a brief chronicle of his research labours, explaining that all material used is available in the public domain in various, and sometimes unusual, locations (e.g. private papers of Lord Caldecote, a name from the British Aircraft Corporation's past). It sounds as if he encountered some resistance in making some of this information more accessible. Considering the impact this catalogue of misdeeds could have, you can imagine why this might be.

The relationships between British arms manufacturers and Saudi Arabia and Iran stand out as perhaps the most prominent in this book, but the influence of the UK arms trade also spreads out far across Europe, and even into Asia. While the details of the transactions underpinning these relationships are generally kept secret, *Deception* reminds the reader of the media fallout when dirty deals have come to public attention, and how companies have avoided convictions thanks to the deliberately abstruse way in which deals are brokered.

My impression was that *Deception* was very statistic-heavy, but these accounts could hardly be presented any other way. When one hundred-million pound figure began to merge into another, I began to appreciate the subtext. Such 'possibly life-changing' sums of money were not only meaningless to me: they were, and are, essentially meaningless to the moguls conducting these deals. The price itself is meaningless, at least – the deals attached stand for security, partnerships between buyers and suppliers, which the suppliers hope will endure. Touches such as the scaling-up of figures from 1970s deals, and the Saudi royal family tree/lists of eminent persons came in very useful.

The use of middleman agents, in countries where suppliers have no firm link with prospective (and often prestigious) buyers, swiftly becomes a familiar element. Almost as swiftly comes the understanding of just how vital a role these agents play – examples illustrate prospective British sales which fell on deaf ears, whereupon another country wangled a deal very soon after. According to Gilby: 'Agents could fulfil a number of legitimate roles … However they were also central to bribery schemes'. This vague possibility of the 'legitimacy' of their services forms part of the obfuscation when attempts are made to prosecute over suspicious transactions.

On a pragmatic level, the commissions these agents receive for helping negotiate a successful contract, generally a percentage of the final selling price, seem predictable given the high-stake nature of these proposals, though the ethics of their services are not as easy to condone. I need not comment on the principles of the industry itself.

On a scale as vast as that of international arms deals, bringing bribery into the proceedings means that many matters besides the basic sale must be attended to. Speaking about 'internal politics within a customer government', Gilby points out how 'if some well-connected people were paid off, and their rivals were not, then the agent's actions could make Britain's relations with some highly influential people very difficult'. So intricate was the game between Britain and Saudia Arabia in the late 1960s that Willie Morris, a British ambassador on the scene, kept information drolly described in the book as a 'Who pays whom' file.

Agents with particular political affinities whom they might support using their commission is another point of interest. The author has diplomatic words to say regarding an agent in Lebanon in the early 1970s, who was a strong supporter of a supposed pro-British electoral candidate in that country: 'Although I have seen no evidence that the British Government was actively trying to influence the outcome of these elections, the commission arrangements were politically convenient.' Plausibly, then, British weapons manufacturers may exert degrees of political influence in places largely unobserved by the British public.

The swift punch of a concluding chapter sums up reams of shady cases from the history of the modern arms trade in a few deeply disheartening pages. Some harsh, memorable juxtapositions in this section suggest that even this comprehensive work only scratches the surface of the issue:

> 'In South Africa, for example, the Government claimed in 1999 [the arms deal described] would cost $5 billion. At the same time, President Thabo Mbeki said South Africa could not afford anti-retroviral medication for the more than 5 million South Africans living with HIV/AIDS.'

Gilby also damns the Western business tendency to play corruption off as 'part of [developing countries'] way of life'; those who would use this phoney attitude as an excuse ignore the existence of anti-corruption laws in Saudi Arabia, and in what could be called the frequent buyer countries. Having said that, we see from *Deception in High Places* that even when suppliers initially defer to the law, their contacts within the country of proposed sale may try to persuade using a variation of this notion, i.e. that all deals brokered use agents anyway, regardless of the official stance.

What surprised me was the assessment of US reform. Gilby rates America as more willing than other nations to provide proof of their work towards reducing corruption. The Organisation for Economic Co-

Operation and Development, a peer review group, produced a 136-page report on steps taken by the US between 1998 and 2011 to bring their dealings in line with recommended policies. For perspective, Britain's was a paltry five pages.

In the case of Britain, the author does not deny that progress that has been made over the years, acknowledging for instance that 'Britain now has one of the strongest anti-bribery laws in the world', and that such developments have been achieved thanks to 'external pressures'; we are to assume, however, that the prospect of creating a conducive mindset within government bodies is a different manner of beast. The number of and scale of the 'scandals' exposed is testimony to this.

Righting where the system has gone wrong is a daunting task. Gilby suggests imposing significant fines on companies operating corruptly, and a reform of ever-suspicious offshore banking as initial steps to reducing underhand practices. Sensibly, he admits that we can never hope to completely eradicate what is essentially a human compulsion, but in order to dissuade powerful entities from it, the penalties imposed must actually pose a threat to the perpetrators' future credibility or financial viability.

Nicole Morris

Absent Genocide?

Ian Barnes with Malise Ruthven, *Crossroads of War – a Historical Atlas of the Middle East*, The Belknap Press of Harvard University Press, 224 pages, hardback ISBN 9780674598492, £25.95

A flamboyant volume indeed, with some hundred pages of brilliant maps and another hundred of history of wars, instruments of war, devastated countries and cultures, incessant assassinations of power holders and their families, mass exterminations, religious intolerance and murderous conflicts, destruction of temples, villages, towns and cities. In a nutshell, war tales of the Middle East, all through the last five thousand years – an impressive scholarly achievement for sure. And all because, as one of the authors explains in the Introduction:

> 'Throughout recorded history the Levantine Corridor has seen the movement of armed forces, as those who controlled this vital strip commanded the whole Near Eastern region.' (p.6)

After reaching the end of the war narratives, and having endured the macabre tales, I somehow felt the need of an Epilogue, to better understand the real and moral *raison d'etre* of such an awesome endeavour, having in mind the turbulent world in which we live. I sincerely wanted to know if the authors, having accomplished their task, do somehow believe or not that another world is possible. And if positively so, I would have felt enriched to know how they envisaged the transformation of that possibility into a probability. In case of a negative stance, then, alas, 'vanity, all is vanity'. The distinguished authors of this unique historical atlas left my queries unanswered.

But then, I remembered a reassuring thought I read in another atlas-book, which had filled my heart with a distilled joy, and a feeling to share it with everyone:

> 'Homo sapiens has been around for at least 250,000 years. Yet war and military might have been known only in the last 5,000 – 2% at most of our history. War is neither a part of human nature nor, necessarily, of civilised life.'
>
> *The Gaia Peace Atlas,* Editor, Dr Frank Barnaby
> Quoted in *Alternative World,* by Nares Craig. (p. 160)

In one of his impressive volumes, Bertrand Russell diagnosed the malaise of power, saying:

> 'Throughout history, great nations have been led to disaster by unwillingness to admit that their power had limits.'
>
> *Has Man a Future?* (p.45)

Crossroads of War totally reaffirms Russell's diagnosis. Regarding both the tragedy of the Jewish people in the aftermath of World War Two, and the diaspora of Palestinian refugees, the authors admit that:

> 'The movement of many people to Palestine, and later the State of Israel, solved some problems for the Jews but, in turn, displaced Palestinian Arabs became refugees, forced to live in camps in other countries where they were not assimilated.' (p. 178)

An apt juxtaposition, for sure, but I remain shocked not to find mention of the word '*Genocide*', when most of the mass and cultural annihilations mentioned by the authors do cry out to be acknowledged as such. It is worth remembering the *raison d'être* of Raphael Lemkin's coinage of the word *Genocide* (see *Spokesman 93*). Lemkin was adamant in saying that *Genocide* 'happened so many times'. Curiously enough, '*Holocaust*' is mentioned once, only to label the Jewish survivors, those who dared survive the magnum crime.

It's worth pointing out that the word *Holocaust* was used during the massacres of the Armenians in the 1890s to underline the religious aspect of the tragedy – Christian Armenians massacred by Moslem Turks and Kurds – as a large mass of Armenians were burnt alive in the Urfa Cathedral in 1895. Hence the word 'Holocaust' was used by the noted missionary, Corin Shattuck, to visualise and characterise this horrible event.

Etymologically, *Holocaust* = *'Whole-Burnt'*, and is intrinsically linked with the act of sacrifice – a sacrificial offering which is completely consumed by fire, whereby cleansing from sins and, ultimately, purification is expected to be attained, functioning as an atonement, or indeed: '*an offering made by fire, of a sweet savour unto the LORD'*. (*The Holy Bible, authorised King James Version, Leviticus*, 1:17)

Does genocide 'taketh away the sins' of the murdered community, whether massacred, gassed or burnt? Or does it, perhaps, cleanse the sins of the murderers for the bliss of purification? God forbid. With all respect to all concerned, it must be said that *Holocaust* is an erroneous and misleading coinage of the reality it is hoped to illustrate and define.

Nazis committed the ultimate crime against humanity, rightly expressed with Lemkin's more precise, politically pristine and religiously unbiased word – *Genocide.*

Perhaps the neglect of the term *Genocide* in Barnes & Ruthven's book is a subtle way of refuting Lemkin's superb trove, especially when the distinguished linguist was adamant to remind us all that in the 20th century *Genocide* happened 'First to the Armenians, then after the Armenians, took action'. (*History of the Genocide,* by V. Dadrian, p. 350)

The Glossary on p.218 of the *Crossroads of War* defines 'Holocaust' as:

> 'Systematic mass murder or genocide of some 6 million Jews by Nazi Germany and its allies.'

Obviously, the authors have cleansed the word *Holocaust* of all its original, religious attributes. When referring to the mass movements of refugees of the Middle East, it is negligent of historical data not to mention the survivors of the Genocide of the Armenians, who were uprooted from their ancestral homelands in Anatolia, as a result of the meticulously planned magnum crime executed by the proto-Nazi government of the Young Turks. Hence, starting in 1915, hundreds of thousands of Genocide survivors became the first Diaspora of Armenians in the Middle East.

This year, 2015, is the 100th commemorative year of that Genocide of the Armenians. Let us hope the authors of this formidable atlas will not be charmed by the zealots of the camp who blindly refuse to acknowledge the veracity of that historical truth.

In the last paragraph of the Introduction to *Crossroads of War*, Malise Ruthven draws a parallel between the Frankish Crusaders, also named as Outremer (from the French '*outre mer*'), and the 'new group of settlers' – meaning the Jewish ones – 'whose project for an occidental state in the Levant carries numerous echoes of *Outremer*' (p. 13). She concludes:

> 'Today a new *Outremer* remains, all-powerful, like its medieval predecessors. But there is no guarantee that in an increasingly hostile environment it can maintain this pre-eminence indefinitely.' (p. 13)

Today's *Outremer* resides not in the Levant, but beyond the oceans – an *Outre-mer* indeed.

Khatchatur I. Pilikian

Benn and the IWC

Ruth Winstone (editor), *The Best of Benn*, Hutchinson, 2014, 260 pages, hardback ISBN 9780091958923, £20

In the late 1960s, the Institute for Workers' Control (IWC) became deeply engaged in providing support to the struggle of those employed by Arnold Weinstock's General Electric Company (GEC) against the mass redundancies this expanding multinational was planning to impose. It had recently been engaged in the takeover of a number of competitors and was determined to impose 'rationalisation' to cut costs.

During the dispute, Tony Benn , Minister of Technology in the Wilson Government, was invited by the management to visit the GEC factories on Merseyside which were under threat. Ken Coates gleefully described at a subsequent meeting of the IWC Council (of which I was Secretary) how Benn had allowed himself to be 'captured' by the shop stewards on site to be shown round the works and given their side of the story. Coates was not only amused but also greatly encouraged by this development. He suggested that Benn might well prove to be a good ally in the developing movement for workers' control and industrial democracy.

We were not used to having good friends in the high places of the political wing of the Labour Movement, so many were very sceptical of Benn's potential to help our cause: at best they thought him to be an able, well-meaning social democrat; at worst, an ambitious careerist.

However, in 1971, with Labour out of office, a storm broke over the Clyde. The Heath Government retreated from Labour's earlier support for reconstituting the shipyards as Upper Clyde Shipbuilders and adopted plans for total rundown and closure. Aware of the recent resistance and occupation of their factories by the GEC workers, and led by imaginative and determined shop stewards such as Jimmy Reid and Jimmy Airlie, the shipyard workers voted to occupy their own yards and work-in to defend jobs.

Tony Benn, now a leading light in the Labour opposition, gave full and enthusiastic support to the UCS workers. It gained enormous publicity and support, and triggered a whole series of sit-ins and work-ins at workplaces, large and small, throughout the land, which were threatened with redundancies. All this upsurge underpinned and fuelled serious radicalisation of the Labour Party. It stimulated the rapid development of detailed plans for the expansion of public ownership, support for workers' co-operatives and compulsory planning agreements with large multinationals, with the close engagement of trade unions.

All this promised a massive extension of industrial democracy. Doubters amongst IWC activists were delighted, even if they had some difficulty in keeping up with Benn in his rapid evolution! Alas, the sceptics were proved right in their doubts about what a new Labour Government might achieve; not because Tony Benn defected from the path of fundamental change or fell short in the determination and commitment it demanded. Far from it! It was the timidity and shortsightedness of the party leadership that took us on another course.

After defeat in the Common Market referendum of 1975, Benn was removed from his key position of Minister of Industry by Harold Wilson. Thereafter, James Callaghan and Denis Healey concentrated their efforts in following the diktats of the International Monetary Fund, confining trade unionists in the ever-tightening bands of the prices and incomes policy.

The selection in this book from Benn's speeches, diaries, articles and so on from his long and rich political life seeks to be representative of Tony's many concerns and involvements with individuals as well as political causes. Ruth Winstone worked closely with Benn for more than 25 years and edited all his published diaries, so she is well placed to have made a good and informative selection. But with such a large field to cover, she is not easily able to convey the excitement of the early '70s when Benn was probably at his most creative. Thereafter, sadly, he became, in the words of the section headings, 'caged' and a 'lost leader'.

Winstone's collection does feature one small piece on UCS and a long extract from his address on workers' control to the Engineering Union in 1971 (reproduced in full in *Speeches* by Benn, recently reprinted by Spokesman). But those who want to know more about the man and his politics need to visit or revisit his diaries and writings. They should be encouraged to do just that and I am sure they will. After all, Tony Benn never turned back. He remained a shining example of cheerfulness and perseverance in the face of adversity. He continued to give people hope and inspiration to the very end.

Ken Fleet